QUANTITATIVE METHODS FOR PLANNING AND URBAN STUDIES

Quantitative Methods for Planning and Urban Studies

BARRY J. SIMPSON
Department of Civil Engineering
University of Aston

Gower

Published by
Gower Publishing Company Limited,
Gower House, Croft Road, Aldershot, Hampshire, England

and
Gower Publishing Company,
Old Post Road, Brookfield, Vermont 05036, USA.

British Library Cataloguing in Publication Data

Simpson, Barry J.
   Quantitative methods for planning and urban studies.
   1. City planning——Great Britain
   I. Title
   711'.4'0941   HT169.G7

   ISBN 0-566-00843-2 /103

Printed in Great Britain

Contents

Preface

A wide spectrum of disciplines share a concern for the urban environment. Town planners, architects, geographers, sociologists, economists, housing and transport officials have a common interest in the built environment and its physical, social and economic effects. All must look to the future to at least some degree and share in deliberate action to bring about desired ends - planning.

In the past, 'planning' has often referred to the statutory town and country planning system, the making of development plans and the control of development. Whilst many other activities with a common concern for the urban environment have also been 'planned' and whilst planning has long since been described as interdisciplinary, the need for concerted action is becoming more and more pressing. The inadequacies of development plans and development control alone to address the problems of the inner city are all too clear. Whilst they may have channelled pressures for development with some effect, when these pressures disappear the statutory planning system is left high and dry. The need to enlist the powers of financial, economic and other agencies to implement policies and projects is clear.

This book is intended for all these disciplines with the common concern for the urban environment and its physical, social and economic effects. It is for practitioners, students and others who wish to further explore methods to help in making decisions. It is concerned with how planning decisions may be assisted by a whole range of techniques, many of them borrowed and adapted from other disciplines.

The scope of planning methods and techniques is indeed wide. Deciding what to leave out has been a problem. Many statistical techniques can be used with great effect and with the wider availability of, and simplification of computing during the last five years or so, these offer much scope for improving decisions. Here, I have included only a few, perhaps enough to encourage some readers to go to the many good books on statistics and think how they can be used in planning.

Developing and applying planning techniques should be much more the product of creativity and rationality than following a set recipe. I have placed much more emphasis on trying to help the reader develop ideas than in listing set procedures. Applying techniques too mechanically, without constant vigilance for what is needed and without looking for effective ways of getting there will lead to a lot of wasted effort and possibly rather obvious results. This is certainly a danger of presenting planning techniques as a set of rigid procedures. On the other hand, a book on techniques must put the question 'how' high in priority. I hope the case studies will help prevent the chapters mainly on principles from appearing completely theoretical.

During the preparation of this book I have been particularly grateful to Mrs Gail Jones of the Department of Civil Engineering at Aston University for setting the type, Mrs Jean Abbott of the Computer Centre for help with the data in chapter 4, and the staff of the University of Aston and City of Birmingham Libraries. Finally, the efficient and courteous way that the staff at Gower have expedited the whole project has been most encouraging.

Dr B J Simpson
Department of Civil Engineering & Construction
University of Aston in Birmingham

February 1985

1 Introduction

WHAT ARE PLANNING TECHNIQUES?

Planning takes on a whole spectrum of meanings. Town planning
as practised in local and central government is certainly
wider in scope than the statutory planning system represented
by the Town and Country Planning Acts. It includes for
example, contribution to housing, industrial renovation and
entrepreneurial activity. Land uses are still a central
interest but the traditional system of making land use plans
and the control of land use changes is inadequate to address
effectively the social and economic issues facing Western
urban areas today. The decline of large industrial cities,
massive unemployment or the environmental impacts of social
and technological change can not be addressed by preparing a
land use plan or by operating a development control system at
the mercy of external economic initiatives to implement. As
Rose (1984) puts it:

> "Adapting metropolitan regions and older areas to economic
> change requires more effective co-ordination with tax,
> fiscal, trade and development policies .... But
> environmental and social concerns will be the binding
> agent."

Planning is carried out by many organisations which
contribute to this urban management. Planning takes place in

most public services by economic and fiscal planners, by
Health Authority administrators, those planning such services
as gas, electricity, water and roads, social services, housing
services, transport services and many more. In the private
sector, planning by firms for their future development is
often in the form of building requirements, almost always in
terms of their financial management and manpower. Chain
stores need to plan their future requirements for land and
premises as do industrialists, housing associations and
building firms, to mention only a few. All of these
organisations and more contribute to planning in the sense of
management of the urban (and rural) systems. Sometimes the
co-ordination is not as effective as it might be. The
statutory land use planning system in the form of structure
and local plans and the need for planning permission is the
central medium for co-ordination but a weak one due to its
ineffective powers for implementation. A review of
relationships between the various disciplines in urban
planning is contained in Khakee (1982).

The form of planning by all these organisations varies in
detail. The subjects being planned for, issues and
constraints differ but are related. The perspectives differ
somewhat but the overall objectives are at least closely
related if not the same. The techniques used across the
spectrum of planning have a lot of common interests. For
example, many kinds of planning in health, economics, town
planning, transport, social services and many other
professions work within requirements set by demographic trends .
and population forecasts. The activity of forecasting is
common to many kinds of planner. Not only are there issues
such as future population and economic activity which are
common to many forms of planning: the methods and techniques
used by planners have even more in common than do the details
of the issues that they face. Similar kinds of techniques are
usable across the spectrum of planning - techniques for
identifying issues, collecting and analysing data and
techniques for assessing their significance for example. All
the techniques considered here can be used where planning has
a spatial element but they are not restricted to it.

'Techniques' is a term which as been applied to many and
varied procedures used by planners. One of the few common
characteristics of all such procedures is that they refer to
some more or less clear cut steps or mode of operation used by
planners to help satisfy a specific purpose that they need to
fulfil, and that they are primarily directed at the question
of how procedures are carried out, the question why having
been addressed largely before the techniques are applied.

Planning techniques seem to fall into four categories according to their origin:

1) Techniques developed by planners with a particular issue in mind, for example threshold analysis, developed to identify alternative sites for house building and to assess the associated costs. Other examples are the goals achieved matrix, the planning balance sheet and the analysis of interconnected decision areas (AIDA).

2) Techniques borrowed and adapted by planners from each other and from other disciplines, for example, cost benefit analysis, input-output analysis, methods of measuring consumers' surplus.

3) Ways of analysing information, used in much the same form in planning as in other disciplines. Most statistical methods including sampling methods, measures of scatter, correlation and regression analysis fall into this category.

4) What are better described as ways of doing their job than as planning techniques - land use surveys, surveys of building conditions and mapping techniques for example. These and the first category are sometimes quite specific to one or more branches of planning.

The term 'technique' is sometimes even loosely applied to indices used by planners such as location quotient to measure the concentration of a specified industry.

All four categories of technique are included here. To some extent the contents of this book have been influenced by what is available elsewhere. There are a good many books on statistics which can be used to gain a theoretical understanding of their derivation. The emphasis here is therefore on practical application to planning situations. There are several good texts, mostly by geographers, on techniques for describing and explaining locations, for example Hammond and McCullagh (1978), Haggett, Cliff and Frey (1977), Cole and King (1968). Description, explanation and prescription (planning) may be regarded as three stages in analysing information, progressively coming closer to decision making. Here we concentrate on the latter stage because these other books are strong on certain aspects of description and explanation.

Is there any difference between planning techniques and

quantitative methods for planning? The four categories just
referred to as planning techniques are a classification
derived from common usage amongst planners in planning
literature. Perhaps there is a slight difference between a
technique and a method in that 'technique' implies a more
formalised, more well-defined and rigid pattern of procedures.
Certainly the fourth category and some of categories 2 and 3
seem to fit more easily into a description as methods rather
than techniques.

Are all planning techniques quantitative? No, there are
techniques for design, eliciting perceptions and a whole
series of methods, if not techniques used in ethnographic
studies. However, we are restricted to those which do rely at
least in part on numerical data, and making explicit the
relationship between them.

PLANS AND POLICIES

Policies seem to fall into two categories. On the one hand
they may explain the way in which an organisation would react
to an external stimulus, for example how a local planning
authority would react to a large number of applications to
convert shops to building society premises, or how a transport
undertaking would react to de-licensing of public passenger
routes. On the other hand, they may explain how an
organisation intends to achieve an objective, for example how
a housing authority intends to improve its dwelling stock or
how a firm of developers selects sites for acquisition.
Policies refer to courses of action, plans specify particular
projects which are to be undertaken, for example plans to
build a metro or a reservoir, plans to acquire and develop
specified sites. Plans of course, ought to reflect policies
but are more specific as to who and what will be affected.
However, a distinction is not always observed. Many documents
referred to as 'plans' for example Structure Plans, are
expected to contain a full range of policies as well as
specific proposals. The ambiguity of usage is not serious.

THE ROLE OF QUANTITATIVE METHODS

Quantitative methods are for testing the feasibility and
desirability of ideas rather than for generating ideas.
Planners must look elsewhere to form their thoughts on what
possible issues might be but statistical techniques and other
quantitative methods can be used to test them. They can be
used to draw out conclusions from data which will confirm or

reject their ideas or show the effects and extent of the issues. Other techniques will help planners to lay out their thoughts in a more systematic way, for example in tracing the implications of a proposal. Others may help to generate alternatives by, for example, defining the spatial possibilities for development, albeit from a limited viewpoint such as that of construction costs. Techniques of evaluation might present a body of reasoning which a planner can apply to form a balanced view, but always the application needs originality of interpretation.

Quantitative methods therefore perform a lot of rather limited tasks in deriving the implications of possible issues or proposals derived elsewhere. Because they are only contributory to making decisions and because they apply to data relevant to a wide variety of decisions, they are quite resilient to change in the role and purposes of planning. Even a radical change to broaden the scope of planning activity which has already started, does not necessarily result in obsolescence of the methods used. The data used and the methods of analysing it are much less subject to change than the scope of the policies they are used for.

ARRANGEMENT OF THIS BOOK

The arrangement has been torn between two conflicting desires. It would have been tempting to arrange successive chapters corresponding to the stages in the process of preparing a plan - information sources, methods of collecting, analysis and so on to monitoring and review. This would have been a neat arrangement to explain theoretical principles, but even more important in view of the literature in this area is the need to demonstrate how planning methods can be applied. Hence most of this book is a series of case studies, each to some extent representing a planning or policy making process in its own right. However, they have been chosen and arranged so as to concentrate on demonstrating techniques and methods in the order they are most likely to be needed in a planning process. And so, the first case study in chapter 4 is selected to demonstrate some common data sources, how to identify and classify issues, how to formulate a research question or hypothesis which can be tested, and some common statistical methods. The survey of attitudes towards housing conditions in chapter 5 is intended to illustrate some methods of data collection including questionnaire design and further statistical methods. Forecasting methods are introduced in chapter 6 in relation to population forecasting, though the same principles are applicable to other kinds of forecasting as well. Techniques for plan generation are explained in the next two chapters, the first concentrating on the main methods of plan preparation, whilst chapter 8 attempts to demonstrate some of the real world practicalities of preparing a plan for a constrained inner city district. Chapter 9, evaluation explains particularly versatile principles in choosing between options in a very wide spectrum of situations. Similarly, chapter 10, monitoring and review, will apply in very similar ways across a range of disciplines.

Before going on to the case studies however, the next two chapters are devoted to explain and raise questions about the principles involved in carrying out research and planning studies. Chapter 2 explains the main stages which may be considered when designing a research study in planning; chapter 3 the main stages in preparing a plan or policy statement. The principles behind carrying out research studies and preparing plans or policies have much in common, but there are also important differences. Firstly, plan or policy preparation is prescriptive. Research studies are explanatory, though it may be only a short step to prescription, and indeed many research studies take this step further. However, the difference in emphasis is evident in the amount of attention paid to implementation, monitoring and review in plan and policy preparation. A second difference is that plans and policies are related to one particular case study - a geographical area for development or improvement, or a policy for a given type of development for example. Research studies try to derive general principles from selected case studies, plans and policies use general principles to apply to case studies. A third difference is that usually there are many more issues in preparing a plan or policy than in carrying out a research study and some of them are at most, only loosely related, especially in plans. Research studies often only have one central issue, though there may be many more closely related to it. These differences in emphasis will be evident from a comparison of the next two chapters, but they certainly do not exclude the transfer of ideas from one to the other.

2 Stages in a research project

There is no pattern to which all good research projects should conform. The stages described here are those which commonly occur in planning and are intended only as a checklist for such projects. A common fault is to inadequately define the subject of the research. Usually the chosen subject includes too much. The first three stages relating to issues, hypotheses and aims should therefore be given close attention early in the project and used continually throughout as a check on the direction in which it is progressing. Often it is best to define the topic first and the case studies later as this gives a better chance of the results applying elsewhere.

1) ISSUES

These are frequently problems, though not necessarily so e.g. studies concerned with taking opportunities such as in identifying areas for the expansion of a town or a site for a factory. Among the questions a researcher frequently asks himself/herself about an issue being investigated are the following:

To whom is this an issue?
Why is it an issue?
Why is it worth attention?

wnat powers are available to take action that may be necessary and who would take the action?

Essentially, identifying an issue means being able to describe a subject which is of concern, defining exactly what it involves so that it can be investigated thoroughly (not for example 'A study of housing associations' or other wide ranging subjects), and being able to argue convincingly why it is significant.

2) HYPOTHESES

These are propositions which are to be tested during the course of the project. They always indicate relationship between two or more concepts e.g. 'Effective traffic control measures are unacceptable and acceptable measures are ineffective'. Often they contain a subject, a course of action and predicted results which are assumed to have a bearing on an issue.

It is extremely important to be careful with the wording of hypotheses. They should be <u>tested</u> during the course of the project (not just <u>supported</u>). Often it is just as valuable to refute a hypothesis as it is to prove it. During the later stages of the project is may be desirable to reword the original hypotheses in view of the evidence which has been available for testing.

Usually several questions can be asked when wording a hypothesis:

- are the cause and the effects each clearly defined?
- can the cause and the effect each be measured or convincingly argued?
- can the relationship between cause and effects be demonstrated?
- what are the alternative explanations?

Examples

<u>Out-of-town shopping centres have caused a decline in local shopping facilities</u> Questions to be asked include:

What constitutes an out-of-town shopping centre?
How large? What kind of goods?
How local are the affected shopping facilities?
Are the effects confined to certain goods only?
How is the decline to be measured? Where is the data to come

from?
What other factors may have caused a decline?
How can you measure these effects? and separate them from the effects of the out-of-town shopping centre?

The best sites for housing have been developed by the private
sector How are the 'best' sites to be defined? least cost?
cost to whom? developer? residents? public authorities?
Intangible considerations. How is the data on construction
costs, costs-in-use e.g. travelling and other factors, to be
obtained?

   How is the private sector to be defined? Are housing
associations to be included?

   The hypothesis may be proved only for some categories of the
private sector (categories defined on size of firm? type of
dwelling? form of organisation?) and refuted for others.

The deterioration in the quality of urban design has been a
direct cause of an increase in vandalism How will you measure
or argue on the quality of urban design? and show
deterioration in selected examples? (presumably by comparison
of examples).
What criteria will your reasoning of quality be based on?
How is vandalism to be measured? litter? graffitti? broken
fittings? structural damage? Are the various forms to be
compared?
How is the 'cause' to be established? Will correlation be a
sufficient demonstration? or will you need to reason on the
motives for vandalism?

The conversion of buildings to offices has resulted in purpose
built blocks remaining vacant Are the occupants (or potential
occupants) of the two kinds of premises similar?
How would you establish who are the potential occupants of an
empty block?
Ask the occupants of a converted building? What other causes
could there be for purpose built blocks remaining empty? How
could you show that they have not had a substantial effect?

Environmental improvement of industrial areas has
substantially stimulated the local economy What kinds of
environmental improvements? Do some have more effect than
others?
How is the success of the local economy to be measured?
Value of product? Employment? Where is the data to come
from?
How will cause and effect be demonstrated?

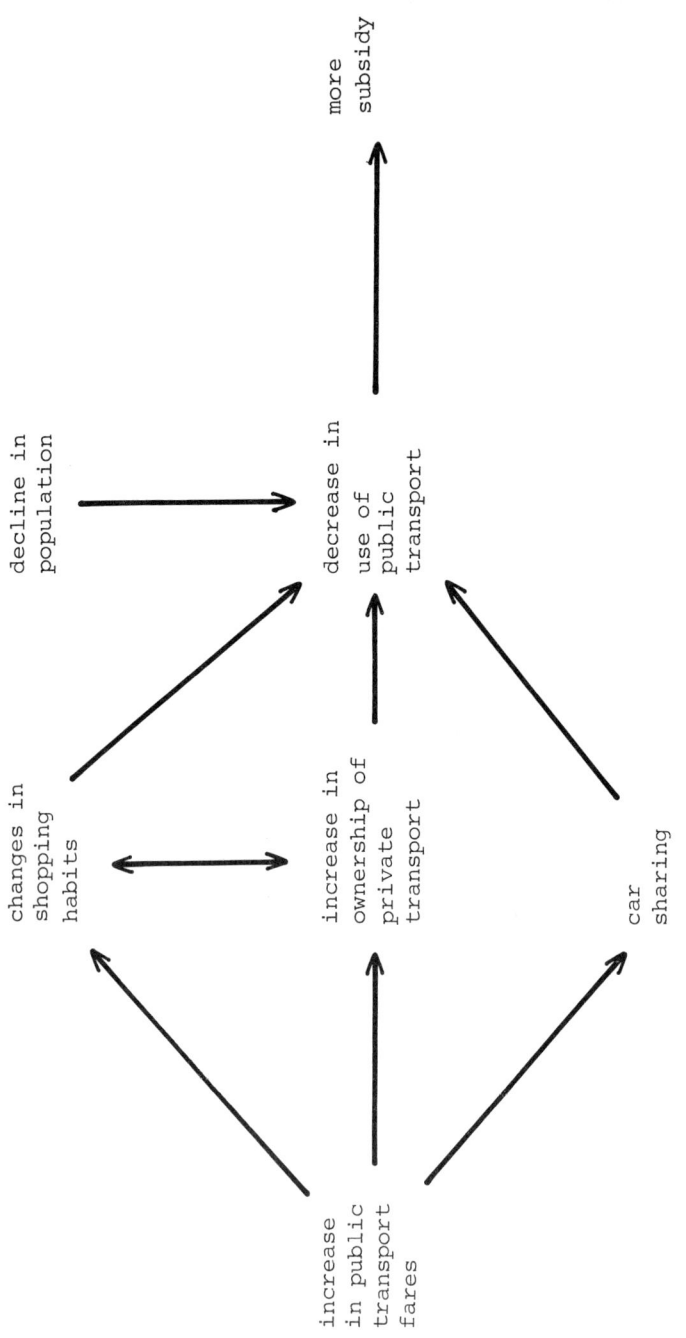

Figure 2.1 Some causes and effects in public transport subsidy

10

Where there is no good reason to expect a particular outcome, a hypothesis may be in the form of question.

<u>Would a review of motorway service station franchises result in less traffic on feeder roads?</u> Are vehicles leaving the motorway for catering and other services? How would evidence be collected? Any particular kind of vehicle?
Is there potential for improvement of services on motorways?
Are operating costs greater? Sufficient to outweigh the larger clientele?
How serious are the effects of traffic leaving and returning to motorways? Serious to whom?

Policies are usually more effective when addressing causes rather than effects. Measures for bringing vacant land into use and for environmental improvements in run-down inner city areas may be inefficient or even a little more than an extravagant use of time and other resources if they do not affect the underlying reasons why the areas are run-down. Unless these causes are addressed the new development may suffer the same fate as the old. Similarly, heavy subsidy of public transport may be an inefficient use of resources if not supported by other measures and policies which affect the reason for the subsidy being needed - perhaps the extensive use of private transport and longer term trends such as a decline in population.

When attempting to address causes as well as effects there is often the problem of how far to trace causes - when to stop asking 'what was the cause of this?' In formulating a policy for public transport subsidy in a rural area for example, possible causes for a decline in usage may be listed including the following:

    decline in population in some age groups
    increased use of private transport
    increased fares
    car sharing schemes
    use of mail order shopping

Some of these factors may have contributed to causing each other. For example increased fares may be helped to increase car sharing schemes and mail order shopping or simply less frequent shopping journeys, more goods being bought on each visit. Soon a network of causes and effects can be traced (Figure 2.1).

The problems are to trace the causes and then to formulate

effective and acceptable measures to address them. If the above example was realistic, a reduction in fares may have some effect. However, other causes such as decline in population would need separate measures, perhaps more investment in employment opportunities, education facilities or other initiatives to make the area more attractive to live in. The problems for planners are that real world networks of causes and effects are extremely difficult to identify (and change through time). Even when they can be acceptably identified, often they would need measures far beyond planning powers and indeed measures which may be unacceptable due to cost, loss of individual freedom, or for political reasons. In reality, planners must tinker with a fragment of such a network of causes and effects. Useful discussions of correlation and how problems of tracing cause may be approached are contained in Marsh (1982) and Atkins (1979).

3) AIMS

These take hypotheses a stage further by introducing an element of action. Often a single general aim can apply to the whole of the project. This can then be expanded into operational aims relating to how the results could be used, methodological aims showing how the project would be carried out and policy aims. The following extract from a recent research proposal by the author to the Economic and Social Science Research Council illustrates this:

"The general aim is to provide those concerned with choice between green-field and urban sites for housing (mainly local authorities, development corporations, housing associations and Central Government) with quantitative information for comparing sites.

In more operational terms there is also the aim to show how the information obtained can be used in decision making and how it can be used in techniques such as cost benefit analysis and threshold analysis by planner and other professional officers.

In order to pursue these general aims, the methodology adopted would be guided by the following:

- to analyse and compare existing data and collect new data on the costs affecting the use of urban sites for public housing.

- to test the significance of this data in order to

12

provide generally applicable guidelines relating costs to site characteristics for example, between orientation and land slope costs, between house type and extra costs according to soil conditions.

In policy terms the research would have the following aims:

- to help clarify the pros and cons of site selection and the arguments on cost appraisal of urban sites. Costs are often overestimated as they ignore the use of existing infrastructure.

- to shed light on the financial arrangements in development including the working of the housing cost yardstick."

Issues, hypotheses and aims therefore all relate to the same subject. Issues identify the subject as a problem or opportunity, hypotheses describe the relationship(s) between the subject and other variable(s) supposed to give rise to the problem or opportunity and aims describe what the research project would try to do about the issues or hypotheses. All are extremely important in defining the scope of a project and a common mistake is to pay too little attention to them, resulting in wasted effort later.

4) MEASURES OR CRITERIA FOR REASONING

The subjects of the hypotheses and aims (which should be similar) need to be translated into criteria which can be measured or argued convincingly. Many planning subjects can not be measured in numerical terms as will be clear from the section on hypotheses above. Sometimes measurements only reflect a part of the subject. For example in the second hypothesis above - How far does 'cost' reflect 'best'? What is cost? Consumers' surplus? Interpersonal comparisons of utility? Time discounting? Evaluation of risk? Subjects which do not lend themselves to numerical measurement can often be analysed rationally. For example, most design topics would involve isolating the criteria for evaluating a design such as variety of form, visual foci and barriers and conformity of components. Even though such a subject does not lend itself to numerical measurement it may still be subject to a large element to rational argument. Some questions which arise at this stage are as follows:

Internal validity - how certain is the researcher that the

causes and effects are related as assumed?

External validity - do the results of the study apply elsewhere? - to other persons and other settings, to other causal factors, would they be found by other researchers?

Contruct validity - how well do the measures of the indicators represent the attribute being investigated? (which can not be defined operationally). How well do the measures represent the subject they are supposed to? Frequently encountered examples of constructs in planning relate to travelling costs, community, inadequate housing conditions and landscape values. What indicators are to be used to represent these? How accurately do they represent these? How can the indicators be measured?

How well do the measurements sample the domain they are supposed to? Do they correlate well with other measures of the same concept? How reliable are the measurements?

Would the test give the same results if applied more than once to the same subject under standard conditions?

Problems of social indicators are discussed in Bulmer (Ed) 1978.

5) PROCEDURES

Research styles may be classified into three basic types, although they usually occur in combination.

Survey usually a large number and range of respondents are involved. Answers are simple and unqualified. Outside effects are controlled by sample selection and/or statistical techniques. This is probably the most frequently used research style in planning. It includes the Census and most types of enumeration e.g. traffic, building conditions, where no control is exerted over any of the variables.

Experimental in which the researcher tries to control all the variables. One or more variables are manipulated to demonstrate the effects on a dependent variable. Experimental traffic schemes such as road diversions or pedestrianisation are examples.

The experimental style is used for testing a causal hypothesis, for example a policy whose effects are uncertain but which does not involve high capital investment.

14

Development control policies are often experimental for review after a short time period to assess the number of applications carried out and their effects. Experiments can also establish qualitative relationships.

Ethnographic which is concerned with a comprehensive explanation of a subject in its natural setting. It deals in reasons and motives and less in statistics and causes than the other styles. It is not a frequently employed research style in planning although some interviews such as those in connections with public participation contain an ethnographic element. It could for example be a style for use in a project measuring the success of specified design elements in a scheme of environmental improvements. Such a project may involve observation (survey) and interview (ethnography). An important strength of ethnograhic research is that the right questions to ask are developed as part of the research itself. The survey style assumes that the questions asked are the right ones - a serious risk and important limitation on surveys.

In order to get a thorough understanding of each of the three styles and the ways they may be complementary to each other, ask yourself which styles may be applied to the six hypotheses in section 2 above.

Research projects in the survey style usually have scope for the use of a wide range of planning techniques. Techniques of plan formulation such as threshold analysis and plan evaluation such as cost benefit analysis are compatible with the survey style and may be usable depending on the subject. Most statistical techniques too, are compatible with the survey style. The relative shallowness of the survey style in terms of the observations on individual subjects, does however make one of the principal pitfalls of many statistical techniques even more serious. Many statistical techniques are much more useful for describing effects than for explaining causes. For example, a correlation may be demonstrable between car ownership and rateable value of housing but this does not prove that one causes the other. Both may be caused by a third factor, perhaps income in this case. Similarly, a correlation between income and distance travelled to work does not tell us which factor caused which, or indeed whether one has caused the other.

The chances of naïve and misleading use of techniques are perhaps greater in the survey style than for experiments. When there is greater control over the variables there is perhaps a greater chance that a correlation really will

Table 2.1

Comparison of Research Styles

	SURVEY	EXPERIMENT	ETHNOGRAPHY
assumptions	many	many	few
scale of application	large	usually small	always small
adaptation to environment	little	little	much
common forms of application	questionnaires, observations, counts	observations	discussions, observations
comprehensiveness of detail on subject	little	little	much
influence of researcher	little	much	little
form of data	quantitative/ descriptive	quantitative/ explanatory	qualitative explana- tions of relationships

Table 2.1 continued

	SURVEY	EXPERIMENT	ETHNOGRAPHY
use of quantitative methods	much	much	little
ability for repetition	great	great	little
degree of description	great	great	little
degree of explanation	little	little directly; some by inference	much
internal validity	high	some doubt	sometimes very doubtful
examples	The Census traffic counts	development control policies; public transport fares changes	interviews e.g. on attitudes; studies on observations of pedestrian movements in shopping centres

demonstrate a cause. At least, in many experiments the variables are manipulated for the purpose of testing causes. For example a change in fares on public transport may reveal a correlation between usage and fares. If change in usage was indeed caused by something other than the change in fares it would be an unfortunate coincidence not intended by the experiment.

Research projects in the ethnographic style lend themselves less to techniques of quantification than do projects in the other two styles. This is due to them usually involving few subjects, lack of standardisation of data collection between subjects and the thoroughness of the way in which subjects are interviewed, which usually results in a lot of non-quantified data. Some techniques which are adapted for non-quantified information may be valuable in ethnographic research. Lichfield's Planning Balance Sheet or Hill's Goals Achievement Matrix may be useful in ethnographic research involving for example, investigation of attitudes. The Analysis of Interconnected Decision Areas (AIDA) may stimulate a researcher's thoughts on ways of setting out ethnographic data.

Forecasts are usually made from data collected by survey. Manipulation of variables as in an experiment may occasionally be valid in forecasting to simulate changes likely to happen in future. A pilot study of fares changes in public transport could, for example, be used to forecast the effect of a more lasting change. Generally however, such control will not be desirable in forecasting. Ethnograhic studies may be useful in forecasting in helping to gain a more enlightened understanding of processes affecting the item on which forecasts are made. In forecasts of usage of public transport for example, a survey would have to rely on a list of questions or items for investigation determined before the survey was carried out. It would depend on being able to ask the right questions. Studies which do no make this assumption - and which would lead to drawing up a list of items for study - would be likely to involve some at least, of the characteristics of ethnographic research.

6) SELECTION OF CASE STUDIES

There are two main criteria for selecting case studies, namely accessibility to data and how typical are the case studies which are available (external validity).

Occasionally, case studies will be selected much earlier

than this stage. Sometimes an interesting case study is the starting point for a project. In fact, in all the stages up to stage 6 it would be difficult to be precise about the topics which need to be addressed without any idea of which case studies are to be used (perhaps as a shortlist). Also, case studies are usually the principal source of data for a research project, and availability of data is one of the essential requirements needed to be able to be sure that a project is viable.

For this reason alone it would be risky to say the least, not to raise the question of selection of case studies before this stage. On the other hand, research projects led by availability of data on a case study are liable to say little of a more general application outside that case study. Such a project would have to trust to luck whether or not any issues of wider application will arise.

The dilemma of whether issues or case studies lead is best resolved by considering both at an early stage of the project. If the idea for a research project is initiated by an interesting case study then it will be wise to ask questions about issues and hypotheses and search for generalities early. For projects initiated by issues it will be wise to check for the availability of data and case studies before proceeding very far. Checking for availability of data however may not mean anything more than drawing up a shortlist of suitable cases, leaving final selection until quite a late stage in the project.

7) DATA COLLECTION AND ANALYSIS

How far will the data test the hypothesis?
Will alternative explanation be revealed?
Obviously a vital part of any project, it is safest to rely only on data which is already known to exist and to be available or that which can be collected within resources available.
Will there be any problems of willingness to respond, confidentiality or access to premises?

This is the stage at which most techniques will usually be applied - techniques of data collection, storage and retrieval (survey techniques in a wider sense than the term as already used), statistical techniques, forecasting techniques and perhaps methods of plan generation and evaluation.

All stages described here may result in some

re-consideration of earlier activities. The results of data analysis in particular may, however, cause some re-wording of hypotheses to make them more testable, which will affect later stages, and some re-thinking of the measures to be used (stage 4).

8)   INTERPRETATION OF DATA AND REFLECTION ON THE RESULTS

What are the weaknesses in the data and interpretation and what else is needed?
What other data should be collected?

A contents checklist for a research report

1) Are the issues, hypotheses and aims clear and plausible?
    What are the subjects?
2) Data collection
        Is the data reliable? (repeatable?)
        Could the researcher or procedure have affected the results?
        Are the scales appropriate?
        Internal, external and construct validity.
        To what other situations would the results apply?
        Are there characteristics of the subject which may prevent this?
        How well was use made of the information obtained?
        Are any further conclusions possible from it?
        How much skill and effort was put into data collection?
        Were any shortcomings avoidable?
3) The results
        What claims are made for them?
        Do the data and analyses justify these?
        Are any alternative hypotheses justifiable?
        Is there anything omitted which would support the claims?
        How original are the results? - original in terms of study area only, setting or original in terms of theory as well?
        What guidance can be given for future research?
        How well is this supported?

3 A planning process

CRITERIA FOR A PLANNING PROCESS

There have been many attempts both in relation to the statutory town and country planning system and by planners in other fields to define a planning process or series of procedures of general application defining the way in which plans can be prepared and put into practice. The journals of the 1960s and early 1970s in particular contain hundreds of examples and there are dozens, if not hundreds, of books which contain an interpretation of the planning process. Many of them are either explanations of how one particular planning study was carried out or theoretical models of an ideal process.

What they have in common is that they reflect their authors' experiences. Planning methods and procedures are best when 'tailor made' to the situation in hand. However, there are principles in their construction and the approach here is to raise some questions for those who may be about to set out on the task of conducting a plan or policy formulation process.

Let us consider some of the characteristics which planning as well as any process of scientific enquiry should possess and what these characteristics mean in relation to the processes by which planning schemes are prepared:

<u>Logic</u> - as far as possible each stage should follow from a substantiated conclusion of a previous stage.

<u>Consistency</u> - the planning process can be seen as a series of stages whereby an almost infinite range of alternatives is checked against criteria relating to what is required. This range is progressively narrowed down and alternatives eliminated until only one or a few are presented for discussion by politicians, public or others responsible for decision making. Consistency means that the criteria for elimination of alternatives should be the same throughout the whole process. In choosing sites for building for example, the criteria for formulating alternatives to choose from should be the same as the criteria for choosing between them.

<u>Efficiency</u> - an awareness should be maintained to direct effort where there is a real choice. For example, which alternatives are likely to be unrealistic for non-technical, perhaps political, reasons? or by reason of an unwilling owner? Which are the choices dependent on subjective, political opinion?

Planning processes are extremely varied. However, all of them address a number of questions:

<u>What needs to be done</u>? Translated into planning terms, this will involve identification of problems, opportunities and issues where there will be a choice between courses of action, together with goals, aims and objectives for the study.

<u>Constraints</u> which restrict the choice of activities possible. What information is necessary? - relating to problems, opportunities, issues and constraints.

<u>The process of assembling information</u> in a suitable form.

<u>Producing conclusions</u> for action; plan preparation from the assembled information.

IDENTIFYING PROBLEMS, OPPORTUNITIES, GOALS AND OBJECTIVES

The need to prepare a plan or policy is usually first mooted as a result of the awareness of an issue or local problems. Industrial dereliction, shortage of land for an urgent purpose such as industry, housing or open space or the need to conserve buildings of architectural interest threatened by redevelopment are all examples of problems which may cause a local planning authority to initiate the preparation of a plan or policy statement. Anticipated changes in usage of services can trigger off plan or policy preparation in other fields. For example, many housing authorities have sought policies for new uses for high rise buildings. Probably less frequently, the realisation of opportunities will initiate plan preparation. For example, a town designated for expansion will usually be the subject of a study involving the finding of sites where advantage can be taken of spare capacities in services and facilities such as schools and health centres. The preparation of many plans, of course, is set in motion by carrying out legal duties such as under town planning legislation, the Transport Acts or by equivalent requirements to anticipate changes in needs in other fields.

Whatever the cause initiating plan preparation, one of the first tasks is to decide goals and objectives, as the aims of a plan are usually termed. A fairly generally accepted difference between goals and objectives is that goals are more generalised statements of intentions whilst objectives state operational procedures whereby goals may be achieved. For example, 'to reduce journey time to work' may be adopted as a goal whereas this may be later translated into the objective 'to allocate land for housing within 3/4 hour journey of employment centres' after housing land availability has been examined. However, this is a distinction by no means universally accepted and in any case, is not of unlimited practical significance. What is important is that an appreciation of feasibility is necessary (as defined above, in relation to objectives) as well as a mere statement of hopes.

Objectives and goals often conflict with each other. These conflicts are where policy choices must be made. They can be clearly set out by means of an objectives compatibility matrix whereby the same objectives are listed as columns and rows to a two-sided table (matrix). Conflicts, such as between providing commerce with transport infrastructure and conservation of the environment, can then be analysed systematically. The Generalverkehrsplan (Traffic Master Plan) for Frankfurt, (Frankfurt-am-Main Dezernat Planung 1976) contains a particularly clear example where goals and objectives are arranged hierarchically and analysed for compatibility.

Identification of problems and opportunities, goals and objectives are all aspects of defining purpose. In some physical sciences it is perhaps more obvious what should be done (if no easier to do it) than is usual in the social sciences, including most branches of planning. This is no doubt the reason for this stage of the planning process being relatively elaborate. Within a local authority planning department this stage will usually involve politician and perhaps public consultation, a list of objectives being presented to planning committee before proceeding further. It will be noticed that objectives contain two facets - a subject of planning concern and a recommended course of action to achieve a desired result. These are exactly the same kind of contents as comprise policies, which are outputs of the planning process. The difference between the two is that policies should be much more precisely defined than objectives and more closely adapted to the peculiarities of the study area. Comparing objectives and policies is an interesting indication of what has been achieved by all the intervening stages of the planning process.

There are relatively few planning techniques in use at this early stage. The more significant ones are those laying out the implications of objectives such as the objectives compatibility matrix and perception techniques for laying out goals (see for example Lynch 1960). Interviews and questionnaires are often used at this stage to identify goals as well as later to compare plans.

COLLECTING INFORMATION AND FORECASTING

Forecasting may be regarded as the conversion of information into a form suitable for use in planning. Much information which relates to the past is only of use as an indication of the future. Information collection is not completed in a short period of time. It occurs at several stages, though it is at an early stage when this is the prime activity rather than being incidental to other tasks. Some information will be necessary very early to identify problems, opportunities and objectives. In fact, Lichfield et al (1975) put data collection and forecasting as activities before the determination of objectives (but after definition of problems). No matter which order is chosen, objectives should be checked against information collected for their feasibility. As objectives also represent aspirations, they should also affect what information is collected. In other words, the process is interactive.

Identifying constraints is a part of collecting information related to the definition of what is feasible. It could for example, include institutional constraints such as the time necessary to carry out essential procedures and their effects on programming.

Many planning and related techniques will be used at the stage of information collection. Sampling methods, questionnaire design, survey design techniques and the majority of mathematical models used in planning will belong to this stage.

ANALYSIS OF INFORMATION

Most of the information collected will need some kind of processing in order to use it for the formulation of policies and proposals. Statistical analysis of data to determine significance, correlation between variables and variance are all methods of showing the usefulness and validity of the information collected and for pointing the way to where more may be needed. Some statistical methods such as sampling will also be used at an earlier stage, in this case prior to information collection.

There are a number of other planning techniques which cover this and some of the subsequent stages of plan preparation, involving the formulation of one or more plans and the evaluation of them. Such techniques include methods of plan generation such as threshold analysis (Kozlowski and Hughes 1972) and evaluation techniques such as cost benefit analysis, the planning balance sheet (Lichfield, Kettle and Whitbread 1975) and the goals achievement matrix (Hill 1968). Other techniques such as input-output analysis will be confined to a shorter part of the plan preparation process. AIDA is also a useful way of laying out information to define alternatives but relies on a considerable amount of information from other techniques as input (Hickling 1974).

PRODUCING CONCLUSIONS FOR ACTION - PLAN AND POLICY PREPARATION

Not surprisingly, this is one of the most elaborate parts of the planning process, and is in fact, usually carried out in at least two main stages: (a) preparation of alternative plans and (b) evaluation of the alternatives to select a preferred one. Often, these stages are sub-divided and/or repeated. Preparation of alternatives may be followed by evaluation, including public or other consultation, followed by further alternatives and evaluation. Sometimes preparation of alternatives may be followed by selection of a preferred plan, followed by preparation of further alternatives based on this single plan, each differing less from the other than did the first set. For example, alternative plans may be prepared for a sub-region on the basis of a different pattern of expansion of the urban area e.g. concentration in a main city, dispersal of expansion to minor centres, new town or linear city linking two or more existing towns. The possibilities are endless. Evaluation may then take place. On concluding perhaps that concentration in the main city is the most feasible, a series of further alternatives may then be formulated differing in terms of direction of expansion. Perhaps a third round may be prepared involving variation in residential densities or different relationships of workplaces and residential areas e.g. dispersed industry, concentrated linear along transport routes.

In a similar way, a transport authority may present a series of alternatives for politician or public comment, based on different modes of transport. If this leads to a decision on the relative investments in perhaps road and rail, further alternatives may be prepared for each mode to show what these investment levels imply.

Plan preparation can therefore involve several stages whereby alternatives are prepared and then tested and then the process repeated perhaps several times. At each round, the issues addressed may be different but the criteria for evaluation and choice should be the same, otherwise there is a danger that an alternative once eliminated could subsequently be shown to be desirable on different criteria. Another danger at this stage is that issues may be insufficiently defined. For example, in determining level of investment in road compared with rail transport it will be necessary to know something of the practical implications of various levels of expenditure. Defining these implications may really belong to a subsequent round of alternatives. These rounds are not as clear and separate as may at first appear.

Presenting alternatives rather than a single plan for public comment and/or professional evaluation has several advantages over presenting just one plan. More meaningful discussion can result from a range of possibilities being available. Most planning studies in recent years have taken the form of a cyclic process in its most liberal sense. For the statutory town and country planning system, the Structure and Local Plans Regulations virtually require this to be the case.

Invariably there is the question of balancing the desirability of having a wide range of alternatives and several stages of preparation against feasibility in terms of data and computational resources available. More alternatives and more stages permit more flexibility and more thorough testing. On the other hand, more time is taken up, plan preparation is delayed and more staff and other resources are necessary.

In striking a balance between resources and speed on the one hand and thoroughness on the other it will be important to consider to what extent the factors influencing choice are matters of public or technical opinion and to what extent they are matters of technical fact. In choosing sites for house building on the edge of a town for example, there may be many intangible questions of landscape damage, loss of agricultural land perhaps loss of open space and effects on neighbouring properties. While so many of the factors to consider are matters of opinion there will be scope for using a wide range of alternative plans and several stages of refinement. If, on the other hand, choice of location for house building rests largely on the choice of the cheapest land in terms of construction costs, then there will be less scope for generating alternatives.

Uncertainty in planning gives rise to a rather lengthy process of plan preparation. Uncertainty relates to both the way in which the present situation can be represented quantitatively and the way it may change in future. Indeed, some would view planning as a process of identifying uncertainty and presenting this for comment to politicians, public and others influencing decisions.

All planning techniques for the preparation of alternatives and evaluation will be used at this stage. Some will also have been used earlier. In town planning, the distinction between methods of plan generation and evaluation is fundamentally one of the number of alternatives considered. Alternative plans ought, collectively, to represent the range of real choices that exist. There may be a large number, depending on the areas of uncertainty. Evaluation techniques on the other hand, are intended to display the pros and cons of a small number of alternative strategies which have been previously prepared. Both types of techniques involve the same kind of factors influencing decisions.

Programming should not be regarded as an activity separate from the methods by which proposals are prepared. A slow rate of implementation, by raising the amount of investment lying idle before returns are realised (frozen costs), may result in a scheme being less attractive than otherwise. Choice between policies and proposals sometimes depends on the rates of realisation which are possible. The methods by which programming can be taken into account, such as critical path analysis and methods of analysing frozen costs tend to be

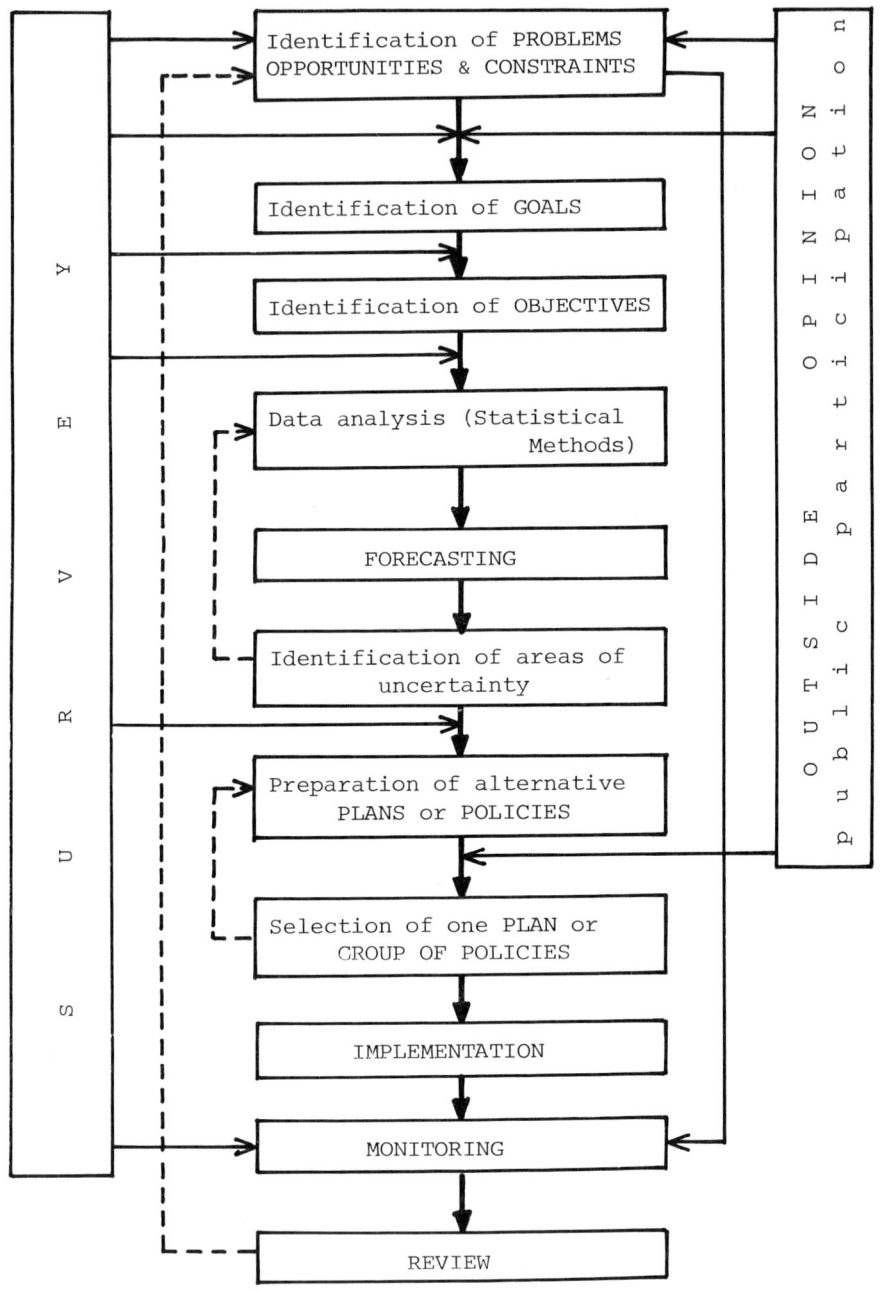

Figure 3.1 A Planning Process

applied separately from other methods involving choice. One
exception to this is threshold analysis.

IMPLEMENTATION

Once it has been decided what policy or plan is to be adopted
there is the task of putting it into practice. Generally at
this stage there is a need to consider three questions - who
is to implement the plan? when? and how? Management
techniques such as critical path analysis and other techniques
based on similar principles help with the latter two
questions. Sometimes the implementation of a policy may be
largely the result of controlling initiatives set in motion by
others. In these circumstances, the techniques for
implementation will overlap with those for monitoring.

MONITORING

This is the procedure by which checks are made on those
factors likely to influence the implementation of a policy to
see to what extent it is being implemented and what are its
implications (in order to see whether the policy should be
changed). There are very few techniques confined to this
stage but several used or other purposes may also be used in
monitoring. For example, several statistical techniques
relating assumed and actual data such as the chi^2 test and
student's t test may be useful. Monitoring also depends on
the updating of information used in techniques applied earlier
- a need to remember when selecting and applying these
techniques.

REVIEW

This is the process of alteration of a policy or plan as a
result of monitoring indicating a need for change. It may
cover any or all of the stages involved in the initial
preparation of the policy depending on the extent of
alteration necessary and therefore any of the techniques in
earlier stages may be re-used.

CONCLUSIONS

There are a number of tasks which generally need to be done or
at least considered as part of a process of plan preparation.
These are summarised in Figure 3.1. They form a framework

which can be used as a starting point for the design of a planning process suited to a particular situation in hand. The stages are far less clearly defined than can be shown in any diagram. There is much more looking backwards to check consistency with what has been found in earlier stages than implied by a diagram. Such a model can at best only give a starting point for creativity in plan design.

After making some progress with the rest of the book, readers may wish to return to the following discussion points on the planning process:

1) To what extent are the stages which can be generally found in these processes common to the relevant professions and disciplines engaged in planning? What are the differences between such planning processes? How might they have arisen?

2) How are subjectivity and creativity catered for in the planning process? For example, is the process relevant to achieving high quality building design?

3) What are the purposes of the process? Is it a conceptually instructive framework to which the use of planning techniques can be related? Is the purpose to explain how all planning activities should relate to each other? or is it a framework on which to hinge involvement of the various parties involved in decision making e.g. politicians, public?

4) How relevant is it to design and how relevant to establishing principles? How relevant is it to the design and layout of buildings on a site which has already been earmarked for development? Is the planning process more relevant to questions of land use rather than density, layout and design?

5) How relevant is it to making decisions on applications received for planning permission (development control)? Does such a process lead to better decisions?

4 Testing a hypothesis using census data

ISSUES HAVE MANY FACETS

As was explained in chapter 2, hypotheses result from issues which are seen as being worth attention. Often hypotheses are more specific than issues. A single issue may initiate several hypotheses more narrow in scope. Sometimes the position is reversed. In this chapter we will look in more detail than in chapter 2 at some of the facets of an issue and a hypothesis resulting from it and some of the complications of trying to test the hypothesis.

An issue such as the concern about educational opportunities raises many questions which must be clarified before it can be investigated with any precision. Politicians, pressure and interest groups and others often refer to equality of educational opportunities as being an aim worthy of pursuit. Presumably they would hope that the opportunities would be equally good rather than equally bad. If the idea of satisfactory educational opportunities replaced equality, this would only beg the question of satisfactory to whom - those being educated? parents? education authority? taxpayers? all of these? What any of these, or any other parties see as satisfactory will be affected by what they think is possible. Their expectations may be open to influence by many factors, perhaps including job prospects, their expected role or position in society or their expectations about relationships with other people for example.

Also, there are many ways of viewing education. The passing of examinations and entry on to further courses has understandably been the first priority at many schools, whilst it has been invariably recognised as being only one criterion of success. Preparation for employment and recently unemployment can be justified without any cynicism by schools which face the reality of many areas. Preparation for migration may be a more positive, if perhaps less realistic attitude.

Opportunities for adult education may be just as important as opportunities at school. They may be vocational, leisure interest or more academic and of almost any level of advancement. Perhaps fortunately, areas depressed in other ways are not always lacking good adult education opportunities. Even the Open University with its 'distance learning' methods, works best where there are substantial numbers of students close together.

When investigating any issue, it will be necessary to ask several questions on why and to whom it is of concern. These will be necessary to establish whether the issue is sufficiently significant to merit investigation and in order to describe and analyse relationships between the various facets of the issue as a first step before formulating hypotheses.

For our issue of educational opportunities there may be many reasons why it should be of concern. Some of the direct consequences of poor educational opportunities may be lack of self-fulfilment, poor job prospects, certain kinds of anti-social behaviour (which may also be a consequence of poor job prospects and other direct effects of poor educational opportunities) and the economic consequences. An educated labour force is a valuable resource. Such direct effects will obviously interact with each other. In addition these direct effects will initiate many indirect effects, perhaps including negative attitudes towards work and towards their relationships within society, and effects on the general decline of a district.

To whom should these effects be of concern? Clearly they will be of interest to schoolchildren, parents and other concerned with the welfare of those who might themselves benefit from education. Also they will be of concern to the education authority and local authority if different, both as providers of education and other services affected by the consequences of it. Central government should share concern for at least the economic, social and educational consequences. Poor educational opportunities may be related to many social problems. Education is also a great liberator, perhaps even the start of some problems. Certainly it seems to have accompanied population movements away from rural and depressed industrial areas. Perhaps the UK as a whole is a net loser by migration. Education also liberates from old ideas, customs and traditions.

A HYPOTHESIS

Only a few of the many possible facets of the issue of educational opportunities have been mentioned. Even these could lead to many different but related hypotheses. One such hypotheses might be that there are spatial variations in the proportions of students staying at school after the age of 16 and also variations between males and females. Obviously this refers to only a very small corner of the issue of educational opportunities. It is, however, an important corner, because it refers to the continuation of full-time education beyond the minimum school leaving age. It might be expected to be a significant indicator of attitudes, opportunities or abilities at an important time of choice in a person's development. The problem for research is that although it may be fair to speculate that the proportion of those staying on at school will be related to such factors as attitudes, opportunities or abilities, it is much more difficult to sort out which of these factors is having most influence. Many studies involving analyses of data from the Census of Population or other information offer little or no explanation of causes, only correlations. Using Census data, we can test for variations from district to district or between the sexes. To offer guidance on causes, reference to other sources or speculation and testing of explanatory variables from the Census will be necessary.

TESTING A HYPOTHESIS

"There are significant variations in the proportions of students at school at the ages of 17 and 18 between the wards in Birmingham and also a significant variation between males and females".

Using a Harris H800 the following file was submitted to the University of Manchester Regional Computer Centre:

Input into file

```
   Type
     JOB (User number),CP76(P5000,TD4,SP)
     LIBRARY (PROCLIB)
     SASPAC (OPCSIN1=WMIDSWDH)
     ####S
     COMMENT
     INPUT SYSTEM FILE 1 NAME=WMIDSWDH
     INCLUDE DISTRICT CN
     TMALE=C1912+C1914
     TFEMALE=C1913+C1915
     MALEST=C1952+C1954
     FEMALEST=C1953+C1955
     EXMALE=TMALE*0.2453617
     EXFEMALE=TFEMALE*0.287021
     INDCHIM=(MALEST-EXMALE)*(MALEST-EXMALE) DIV EXMALE
     INDCHIF=(FEMALEST-EXFEMALE)*(FEMALEST-EXFEMALE)
                                           DIV EXFEMALE
     STDEVM=(MALEST/TMALE-0.2453617)*(MALEST/TMALE-0.2453617)
     STDEVF=(FEMALEST/TFEMALE-0.287021)*(FEMALEST/TFEMALE
                                             -0.287021)
     LIST VARIABLES TMALE TFEMALE MALEST FEMALEST EXMALE
               EXFEMALE INDCHIM INDCHIF STDEVM STDEVF
     END
     FINISH
     ####S
     ****
     $EOF
```

Sending the job

   Type (institute code) (filename)

Some points of explanation

SASPAC(OPCSIN1) refers to the Small Area Statistics Package of
the Office of Population Censuses and Surveys for the 1981
Census of Population held at the University of Manchester
Regional Computer Centre(see UMRCC 1982).

WMIDSWDH refers to the West Midlands Ward data at hundred
percent level.

CN is the code for Birmingham
TMALE is total male population
C1912 and C1914 = males aged 17 and 18
C1913 and C1915 = females aged 17 and 18
FEMALEST are female students

C1952 and C1954 = male students aged 17 and 18
C1953 and C1955 = female students aged 17 and 18
EXMALE is the expected number of male students if each ward
  had the same proportion
0.2453617 is the total number of male students aged 17 or 18
  resident in Birmingham (4,351) divided by the total
  number of male residents aged 17 or 18 (17,733)
0.287021 is the total number of female students aged 17 or 18
  resident in Birmingham (4,989) divided by the total
  number of female residents aged 17 or 18 (17,382)
INDCHIM is the (observed-expected)^2 divided by expected
  male students
STDEVF is the (deviation in proportion of female students)^2
  for each ward

Output from the computer consisted of:
- total number of males aged 17 or 18 for each ward
- total number of females aged 17 or 18 for each ward
- total number of male students aged 17 or 18 for each ward
- total number of female students aged 17 or 18 for each ward
- expected number of male students aged 17 or 18 for each ward
  (total number of males aged 17 of 18 multiplied by the
  average proportion of males of these ages staying at school
  i.e. 0.2453617)
- expected number of female students aged 17 or 18 for each
  ward
- (observed-expected)^2/expected male students. Summing
  these gave a chi^2 value of 678.573 including all the wards
  in Birmingham with 41 degrees of freedom. Inspection of a
  table of chi^2 values will reveal this to be signficant at
  greater than 99.5% level i.e. we can be more than 99.5% sure
  that the distribution of males staying at school at the ages
  of 17 and 18 is uneven.
- (observed-expected)^2/expected female students. Summing
  these gave a chi^2 value of 660.413 including all the 42
  wards in Birmingham with 41 degrees of freedom. Inspection
  of a table of chi^2 values will reveal this also to be
  significant at greater than 99.5% level i.e. we can be more
  than 99.5% sure that the distribution of females staying at
  school at the ages of 17 and 18 is uneven.
- (the deviation in proportion of male students)^2 for each
  ward. Adding these for all wards and dividing by the
  number of wards (42) gives the variance. The square
  root of this is the standard deviation (0.0985616). The
  standard deviation for females was similarly calculated to
  be 0.1038888.

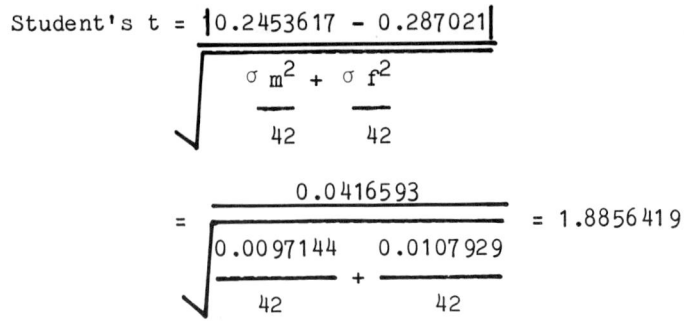

$$\text{Student's } t = \frac{|0.2453617 - 0.287021|}{\sqrt{\dfrac{\sigma_m^2}{42} + \dfrac{\sigma_f^2}{42}}}$$

$$= \frac{0.0416593}{\sqrt{\dfrac{0.0097144}{42} + \dfrac{0.0107929}{42}}} = 1.8856419$$

With 41 degrees of freedom, inspection of a table of student's t values reveals this difference to be significant at a level between 95% and 97.5% i.e. we can be between 95% and 97.5% sure that there is a tendency for more females to stay at school at the ages of 17 and 18 than males.

The results were influenced by three decisions concerning the methods used. Firstly there was the choice of the ages of 17 and 18 to represent people staying on at school. This is not a precise reflection but is the nearest possible within the scope of the Census data. The second decision was the choice of study area. The City of Birmingham is a local education authority. It contains the core and inner surburbs of Birmingham though some of the middle suburbs to the west are within Sandwell Metropolitan District and some of the outer suburbs, especially to the south-east are within Solihull Metropolitan District. Some of the most prosperous residential areas in the West Midlands are thereby excluded from the main city towards which they look (sometimes reluctantly). Had they been included, it is very likely that the chi^2 values would have been even higher. On the other hand, another prosperous and fairly independent town which is included within the City of Birmingham administratively is Sutton Coldfield to the north. Had this been excluded, the chi^2 value for males would have been 424.301 and for females 399.755 with 38 degrees of freedom in each case (still more than 99.5% significant).

A third decision concerning the methods used which affected the results was the choice of wards as the data units. Wards are the administrative unit nearest in size to secondary school catchment areas. There was in 1981 an average of 104 male students aged 17 or 18 and 119 female students which by implication corresponds to the sixth-form age group, although the boundaries do not coincide with school catchment areas. Where supporting studies are available it may be feasible to substitute districts of common social and economic characteristics for wards. This may be attempted using Census enumeration district data, although again, some decisions would be arbitrary and could lead to suspicion of the results. In the present study, the chi^2 value was so clear that the results did not seem to be in doubt.

Only 5 of the 42 wards had a greater proportion of male 17 or 18 year old students than female. The significant difference shown by the student's t test was therefore not unexpected. In fact, the likelihood of chance being the cause of a ratio of 5:37 for highest proportion of male students to female students can be calculated from the binomial distribution:

$$(a+b)^n = a^n + n\ \frac{a^{n-1}b + n(n-1)a^{n-2}b^2}{1!} + .. + n(n-1)..(n-r+1)a^{n-r}b^r .. + b^n$$

If the ratio 5:37 was pure chance, then the probabilities of male students being in the highest proportion and female students would be equal i.e. both a and b would equal 0.5.

The chances of a ratio of 5:37 happening under these circumstances can be calculated as twice:

$$0.5^{42} + \frac{42 \times 0.5^{41}\ 0.5}{1!} + \frac{42.41 \times 0.5^{40}\ 0.5^2}{2!} +$$

$$\frac{42.41.40 \times 0.5^{39}\ 0.5^3}{3!} + \frac{42.41.40.39 \times 0.5^{38}\ 0.5^4}{4!}$$

$$+ \frac{42.41.40.39.38 \times 0.5^{37}\ 0.5^5}{5!}$$

which is small enough to defy a recording on most pocket calculators.

The binomial distribution leads us to believe that the chances of there being no significant difference in the proportions of males and females aged 17 or 18 at school are even less than student's t suggested. However, the binomial distribution relied on dichotomous data (which sex had the highest proportion of students in each ward). The student's t test used cardinal data and for this reason can be expected to be more reliable.

CONCLUSIONS

Both parts of the hypothesis were phrased so that they could be tested using 1981 Census information - "There are signficant variations in the proportions of students at school at the ages of 17 and 18 between wards in Birmingham and also a significant variation between males and females". To be of practical application, it will be necessary to explore the reasons why this is so. Each possible reason may then be examined in turn and evidence collected to establish its validity or otherwise. For example:

- Variations in the number of sixth-form places available. This is quite easily testable.
- Variations in ability of students. Performance in examinations could be quite easily established, but many other factors as well as ability of students could affect this.
- Teachers' attitudes and abilities. Teachers' qualifications and experience might not be very difficult to find out but this would not be a very reliable indicator of ability and even less reliable as an indicator of attitudes.
- Parental attitudes.
- Job prospects. Local vacancies will give some guidance but employees' willingness to travel may be unknown. Also, it is students' perceptions of job prospects which may affect their attitudes towards education and these perceptions may be different from reality.
- Students' attitudes, influenced by many other factors.

The testing of a hypothesis such as the present one is only the starting point of a series of further studies (or the end if it reveals them to be unnecessary), some of which can make use of existing data, some will require surveys or observation of attitudes.

Sometimes, other supporting data may be extracted from the Census. This contains population variables including numbers and ages, sex, marital status, those in employment, country of birth, socio-economic group, sector of employment, means of travel to work, household composition and car ownership. It also contains some variables on housing conditions - dwelling type (house, flat etc.), tenure, size (household and dwelling) and presence of amenities (bath, inside w.c., self-containment). The data used in this study was by wards (local government districts). Perhaps more commonly used in planning

are enumeration districts. These are the small areas covered
by each enumerator at the time of the Census, with on average,
a population of around 500 in urban areas and 150 in rural
districts. These are the smallest areas for which Census
information is available, and they permit a lot of flexibility
to aggregate them to form areas for planning purposes. A full
account of the contents and methods of analysing Census data
is Rhind (1983).

5 Questionnaire design and analysis

A QUESTIONNAIRE SURVEY ON HOUSING ATTITUDES

A questionnaire survey was carried out in Sparkbrook, an inner suburb of Birmingham, in an area of late nineteenth century terraced housing which was largely unimproved but was generally in such condition as to qualify for area improvement and renovation grants. It contained 210 dwellings with a substantial amount of light and general industry and warehousing in buildings of the early twentieth century the 1960s and 1970s.

The two main issues to investigate were firstly whether the future of the area was for housing, industry or both. Some of the industrial premises were less than 20 years old and it seemed unlikely that there could be a case for removing them. The second main issue was that if there was a future for housing, then what sort of treatment, if any, should it receive? - limited external improvements by the Council free of charge to all dwellings terrace by terrace (the 'Envelope Scheme')? other forms of area treatment such as housing action area or general improvement area? or continuation with the award of renovation grants on a house-by-house basis?

The questionnaire was delivered through each letter box and was collected a few days later. Up to three calls were made where there was no reply at first. 107 questionnaires were collected complete. A further 24 were completed by interviewers by personal interview with the respondents in cases where they did not have the questionnaire to hand. The results of these were analysed separately from the remainder to check whether the interviewer had had any influence on the answers. The questionnaire used, and the results for all 131 replies were as follows:

"I am a student at Aston University and I am helping to carry out a survey of this district to find out opinions on housing conditions. Would you mind answering a few questions on what you think of the housing in the streets around here?

		YES	NO	DO NOT KNOW
1.	Do you know that the Council is thinking of offering to improve the houses in this street?	37	93	1
2.	Do you want the Council to improve them?	104	17	10
3.	Do you think the Council should improve any of these in the area?:			
	a) pavements	107	14	10
	b) parking spaces	74	34	23
	c) shut off some roads	56	59	16
	d) play spaces for children	96	4	31
	e) tree planting	68	42	21
	f) could you say which is most important by writing 1 against the most important, 2 against the second, and so on?	pavements parking spaces shut off some roads play spaces tree planting		
4.	Do you think your house needs any of these?			
	a) new bathroom	51	56	24
	b) water heater	30	87	14
	c) new plumbing	45	62	24
	d) roof repairs	48	27	56
	e) damp treatment	44	63	24
	f) garden wall	51	60	20
	g) garage space	63	51	17

Figure 5.1   Stratford Road is the main focal point of
Sparkbrook as well as being one of the principal
radial routes of the whole City of Birmingham.

Figure 5.2   Ladypool Road, Sparkbrook, a busy local shopping
centre providing a wide variety of goods from
independent shops as well as national chain shops.

5. Would you like the Council to carry out any of the following improvements to your house free of charge?
   a) new roof   78   30   23
   b) new windows   94   20   17
   c) garden walls   51   66   14
   d) cleaning the brickwork and
      pointing   108   20   3

6. If they did, would you be willing to contribute 25% towards the cost of improvements to the inside of your house?   37   41   53

7. Are the industries around here a nuisance?   40   82   9

8. What do you think should happen to the industries in the streets around here?
   a) should they move out so that
      the area can become residential?   32   91   8
   b) should they be allowed to
      expand so long as they do not
      cause a nuisance?   57   43   31
   c) should they remain as they are?   72   34   25

9. Do you think the Council should try to reduce traffic on the residential streets here?   36   72   23

So that we can use the answers you have given me, would you mind answering a few questions about your family and your house?

	less than 35	35-60	61 or over
10. Which age group are you in?	41	62	28

	husband	wife	children	others
11. Do you have a family living with you?	51	67	326	48

	rent	own
12. Do you rent or own your house?	82	49

43

Figure 5.3 Sparkbrook: basically sound late Victorian terraces, many houses having been improved with grants; some local shops still survive.

Figure 5.4 Some terraces will be cleared. New uses have been found for old premises as the social and cultural characteristics of Sparkbrook have changed.

	flat	house
13. Is it a flat or house?	44	87

	1-3	4 or more
14. How many rooms do you have? (counting only living rooms, bedrooms and kitchen)	42	89

15. How long have you lived in this
part of Sparkbrook?   number of years .....

	YES	NO	DO NOT KNOW
16. Are you generally satisfied with the district as it is?	58	52	21

In addition the following were noted by the interviewer when collecting the questionnaire.

	M	F
sex of person filling in questionnaire	61	70

racial origin UK or European 23, Asian 72,
West Indian 27, Other 9

SOME METHODS FOR ANALYSING THE RESULTS

The results may be analysed in relation to the two main issues.

A) Is the future of the area for housing, industry or both?
A first impression of attitudes towards industry can be seen from the answers to questions 7 and 8, for housing questions 2, 3 and 5 and the present mixed uses question 16. Further indication of the value of the results can be obtained by checking for consistency in the answers. For example, similar results may be expected for questions 7 and 8a). However, it is not sufficient to compare the results as described above. They give us no indication of whether the same respondents answered yes or no to both questions or whether they answered yes to one question and no to another. The find this out we need to go back to the original questionnaires. Disregarding 'do not knows' as being inconclusive we can construct a table as follows:

Figure 5.5   Small scale industrial premises of recent decades
have been built into the Victorian grid pattern.

Figure 5.6   Some larger industrial premises are located near
the canal and railway, although at present they
rely more on roads never intended for them.

```
                        Nuisance?
                   | YES    NO  |
                   |            |
Move out?   YES    | 28     2   |  30
            NO     | 10     75  |  85
                   |  38    77  | 115
```

The correlation between the answers can be checked using
the Phi coefficient

```
                        X
                  |  1        0   |
      _____ |_____|_____
                  |               |
  Y        1      |  a        b    |    a + b
           0      |  c        d    |    c + d
      _____ |_____|_____
                  |               |
                  | a + c    b + d |      n
```

phi coefficient   = $ad - bc$

$$\sqrt{(a+b)\ (c+d)\ (a+c)\ (b+d)}$$

In our case this is $\dfrac{(28 \times 75) - (2 \times 10)}{\sqrt{30 \times 85 \times 38 \times 77}}$

$= 0.7615$

In this case $chi^2 = \dfrac{n\ (|ad - bc| - n/2)^2}{(a+b)\ (c+d)\ (a+c)\ (b+d)}$

$= \dfrac{115\ (2080 - 57.5)^2}{30 \times 85 \times 38 \times 77} = 63.0561$

If the chi^2 is significant then so too is the phi
coefficient. With one degree of freedom the chances of
the null hypothesis being correct are exceedingly small
therefore the correlation is signficant.

In this case answering yes to the nuisance question was
paired with answering yes to the question on moving out.
If a yes answer had been paired with a no, then an equally
strong negative correlation would have resulted.

B) If there is a future for housing, what sort of treatment
    should it receive?
    Questions 3, 4 and 5 address the alternative forms of

Figure 5.7   Much pre-1914 housing in Birmingham has now been
renovated as part of a General Improvement Area,
or as here, Housing Action Area and Envelope
Scheme.

Figure 5.8   Under the Envelope Scheme, Birmingham City Council
provides external improvements to the housing
fabric block by block (Brunt et al 1982).

housing treatment. Questions 4 and 5 in particular reflect existing conditions at least as much as preferences. All the items in question 3 are poorly provided and therefore the results may be expected to relate more closely to preferences than result from differential inadequacies in the area at present.

In such circumstances it will be appropriate to test for differences in the results. For example, are parking spaces preferred to tree planting? Is the difference between results significant?

	YES	NO	DO NOT KNOW	
parking	74	34	23	131
tree planting	68	42	21	131
	142	76	44	262

Using the chi^2 test, observed frequencies are as above, expected frequencies as follows for parking and tree planting:

$$\frac{142 \times 131}{262} + \frac{76 \times 131}{262} + \frac{44 \times 131}{262}$$

YES   NO   DO NOT KNOW

Expected	YES	NO	DO NOT KNOW
parking	71	38	22
tree planting	71	38	22

$$chi^2 = \sum \frac{(0 - E)^2}{E}$$

$$= \frac{3^2}{71} + \frac{4^2}{38} + \frac{1^2}{22} + \frac{3^2}{71} + \frac{4^2}{38} + \frac{1^2}{22}$$

with 2 degrees of freedom (3 columns - 1) x (2 rows - 1)

$$= 1.1865$$

Inspection of the chi^2 distribution will show this result to be inconclusive. Similarity of opinions towards parking and tree planting has not been proved.

The number of degrees of freedom is the number of frequency values which it is possible to assign arbitrarily. If a population of n observations is grouped into x classes, after (x-1) classes have been determined then the last one follows from the total. Where the data refers to pairs, the degrees of freedom are reduced to (x-2). Remember that in the chi^2 test you are testing whether two populations are significantly different. The number of degrees of freedom is the number of ways in which individual cases could differ yet the totals and means be unaffected.

Consistency of opinions between different groups within the study area can be tested by comparing ranking using Spearman's Rank Correlation Coefficient. For example, are the opinions expressed to question 3(f) similar throughout the study area? To test for this, the study area would have to be divided into sub-areas (perhaps streets) and data assembled for these:

	A	B	Difference Di
pavements	1	1	0
play spaces	2	3	1
parking	3	4	1
tree planting	4	2	2
shut off some roads	5	5	0

Are the people of sub-areas A and B expressing significantly different priorities?

$$\text{Spearman's Rank Correlation Coefficient} = 1 - \frac{6 \sum Di^2}{n(n^2 - 1)}$$

$$\text{In this case it equals} \quad 1 - \frac{6 \times 6}{5 (5^2 - 1)}$$

$$= 0.70$$

The value of Spearman's Rank Correlation Coefficient can be interpreted by reference to the equation

$$z = \text{correlation coefficient} \sqrt{n - 1}$$

where z refers to the area of the normal curve in standard deviations, and n is the number of pairs of data

$$z = 0.70\sqrt{4} = 1.40$$

Reference to the normal curve shows that this does not reach the value of $z_{0.005} = 2.58$; no significant correlation has been shown.

It may be of concern to find out whether some of the personal characteristics in questions 10-16 vary within the study area. For this purpose, the study area may be divided into sections and then student's t test may be used to show whether they are different. For example, the study area was divided into two sections, A and B. and the answers to question 15 (period of residence) analysed for each as follows:

Section A. The mean period of residence in years was calculated (by dividing the sum of all the years of residence of each respondent by the number of respondents) and found to be 5.2 years. The standard deviation was calculated by measuring the difference of each individual answer from the mean, squaring this difference, adding these squares for all 48 respondents, dividing by the number of respondents (48) and taking the square root of the whole. In terms of formula this is as follows:

$$\sigma = \sqrt{\frac{\sum (x - \bar{x})^2}{n}}$$

where n is the number of respondents
      x is each individual answer
      $\bar{x}$ is the mean length of residence

The same procedure was repeated for section B.

Student's t may be calculated from the following formula:

$$t = \frac{|\bar{x} - \bar{y}|}{\sqrt{\dfrac{\sigma x^2}{n_x} + \dfrac{\sigma y^2}{n_y}}}$$

mean $\bar{x} = 5.2$ $\bar{y} = 6.8$
standard deviation $\sigma_x = 3.1$ $\sigma_y = 3.2$
number of cases $n_x = 48$ $n_y = 33$

$$t = \frac{|5.2 - 6.8|}{\sqrt{\dfrac{(3.1)^2}{48} + \dfrac{(3.2)^2}{33}}}$$

$$= 2.2393$$

The number of degrees of freedom is $48 + 33 - 2 = 79$.

We see from a table of the Student's t distribution that this lies between 97.5% and 99% levels, therefore we can be more than 97.5% sure that there is a significant difference between the two sections.

Sometimes it is useful to compare samples to find out whether there is a significant difference. For this purpose, Snedecor's variance ratio test may be used. Suppose we wish to compare section A for Sparkbrook with another sample of 30 with a mean of 6 years and a standard deviation of 3.4 years

	section A	sample
mean	5.2	6.0
σ	3.1	3.4
n	48	30

Do the standard deviations vary significantly? In section A there is a sample variance of $(3.1)^2 = 9.61$ with $48 - 1 = 47$ degrees of freedom.

Let us test the hypothesis that both section A and the sample come from the same population.

Applying Bessel's correction

$$\hat{\sigma}_1^2 = \left(\frac{n_1}{n_1 - 1}\right) s_1^2 = \frac{48}{47} \times 3.1^2 = \text{lesser estimate of population variance}$$

Similarly, for the sample

$$\hat{\sigma}_2^2 = \left(\frac{n_2}{n_2 - 1}\right) s_2^2 = \frac{30}{29} \times 3.4^2 = \text{greater estimate of population variance}$$

$$F = \frac{\text{greater estimate of population variance}}{\text{lesser estimate of population variance}} = 1.2184686$$

On examining tables of variance ratios at the 5% and 1% levels we see that the calculated value of F is less than both these levels and it is to be concluded that the difference between standard deviations in not significant.

When there are two samples of size n and n and with means m_1 and m_2 the standard deviation of the population can be estimated as follows:

$$\sigma^2 = \frac{(n_1 - 1)\sigma_1^2 + (n_2 - 1)\sigma_2^2}{n_1 + n_2 - 2}$$

$$\sigma^2 = \frac{(47 \times 9.61) + (29 \times 11.56)}{76} \qquad \sigma = 3.2178$$

$$t = \frac{|m_1 - m_1|}{\sigma\sqrt{\dfrac{1}{n_1} + \dfrac{1}{n_2}}} = \frac{|5.2 - 6.0|}{3.2178\sqrt{\dfrac{1}{48} + \dfrac{1}{30}}} = 1.0682$$

The number of degrees of freedom is 48 + 30 - 2 = 76.

Inspection of Student's t distribution will reveal that a signficant difference between the sample and section A has not been proved.

These of course are only a few of the statistical tests which could be applied to the data, chosen partly to demonstrate a variety of methods. There are many useful sources for further reading. Some of the most useful for the social sciences are Yeomans (1968), Blalock (1972), Young and Veldman (1972) and Wright (1979).

ISSUES IN DESIGNING AND ADMINISTERING THE QUESTIONNAIRE

1. Questions were related to the issues identified before the survey. No open-ended questions were asked which could have been aimed at finding out whether there were any other issues.

2. Open or closed questions? All those used were closed.

Open questions have the advantage that there is no assumption made by the survey as to what is important to the respondent. Answers to closed questions are always liable to be irrelevant because the questions were the wrong ones. However, closed questions help to explain the scope of the survey. For example, the improvements listed in questions 3, 4 and 5. Open ended questions (for example 'What improvements do you think the Council should do in this area?') would have given no indication of what might be possible.

3. Personal questions (10 onwards) were put at the end. The relevance of these is not always quite so obvious to the respondent and therefore they were asked after the interviewer had had a chance to explain the scope of the survey in the course of asking the earlier questions.

4. Rather large categories were used for some questions such as age (question 10). This was to reduce the chances of causing offence in sensitive questions especially where precision was not vital.

5. Some data, such as racial origin or sex, can be obtained by observation. Other data such as rateable value can easily be obtained elsewhere.

6. Categories used in questions such as 3, 4, 5 and 6 were related as closely as possible to improvement schemes and regulations in the legislation.

7. The questionnaire was delivered through letter boxes and collected several days later. This way the interviewer could help those having difficulty in filling it in and thereby achieve a higher rate of reply. Those where substantial help was given were kept separate from the rest so that they could be tested to see whether the results were different.

8. Questionnaires are not always only for the purpose of obtaining information. They can also be a means of giving information to the respondent for publicity or public relations purposes. Question 1 was mainly for this purpose. Other questions also had a dual purpose.

Further discussion on questionnaire design is contained in Oppenheim (1966), Gardner (1978) and Nachmias and Nachmias (1981) and on sampling methods for surveys in Zarkovich (1965) and Yates (1981).

6 Forecasting

WHAT DO PLANNERS NEED TO FORECAST?

For many planning purposes it would be even more interesting
to know what is likely to affect planning in future than what
affects it at present.   Forecasting the needs for buildings
and land uses is not suprisingly of vital importance to
planners.   Requirements for any land use or building which
they can control or any important factor affecting such a
requirement can be a subject for forecasting. To simplify the
task to manageable proportions however, it is often assumed
that three basic subjects for forecasting will give a good
indication of the the requirements for others:

- Population total has an important bearing on all activities
  though it is certainly not the only determinant.   Some
  requirements such as for schools will be very closely
  related to future population in the relevant age groups.
  Other requirements such as for housing will be influenced
  greatly by other factors as well - in this case by household
  formation rates and all the social and economic factors
  which in turn affect these formation rates.   Similarly,
  shopping facilities, sports, caravan parks and many other
  uses will not necessarily be greatly affected by population
  totals.

- Housing, itself influenced by population amongst other

factors. The location of housing has a decisive influence on the need for a whole host of other uses which must be provided close to it - schools, some kinds of shops, libraries and other community facilities for example.

- Places of employment, perhaps influence population movement both at a national scale and more locally. The location of factories and offices certainly have a profound influence on transport patterns and probably also on car ownership.

If these three basic items could be estimated then we would certainly have a good start towards knowing requirements for a number of other land uses and activities. There are however, certain other uses which are known to be quite independent of these. Shopping floorspace requirements are perhaps the most important exception in commercial terms. Shopping habits are thought to depend on many factors other than population totals, and the location of home and work. Disposable income, transport facilities and simply habits and fashion (the image created by many stores for example) are all thought to be influential by those companies who invest in shopping centres, so much so that the forecasting of future shopping requirements has developed almost as an independent activity by specialists in the field. Relationships between forecasts and methods of integration are reviewed in Breheny and Roberts (1978). Forecasting of course, is a task undertaken in many kinds of planning - by economists, and those engaged in energy requirements, health services, and transportation only to mention a few. Some of their work has much effect on the work of town planners and some of the methods used and constraints experienced are similar (Ascher 1978).

FORECASTING TRENDS OR THE EFFECTS OF POLICIES?

When forecasting all these activities, are we concerned with what would happen in the absence of intervention by local and central government? (in which case we would be forecasting something which we do not expect to happen), or are we trying to forecast what actually will happen? (Presumably planners hope that there will be progress towards stated aims via policies and proposals, hence forecasting and plan preparation would seem to be much the same). Are we forecasting demands or supplies? One way out of this apparent paradox, is to think in terms of trying to forecast pressures that will tend to make a policy or proposal deviate from its desired course. Planners are trying to forecast what opposition their policies and proposals will meet from events and trends - opposition that makes them harder or easier to implement and opposition that will raise questions about whether the policies and proposals should be changed. Further discussion is contained in Bracken (1982).

FORECASTING ACTIVITIES SEPARATELY

Often, forecasts are made for population and each land use separately. Yet they are so clearly interdependent that there is a real danger of each type of forecast being dependent on the others. A circular argument results where each forecast is dependent on assumptions made elsewhere. It is therefore tempting to think of forecasting in terms of a systems view of land uses and activities using a comprehensive approach, quite opposite to the currently favoured view in other branches of planning favouring an incremental, problem solving approach. Perhaps here, the theory of forecasting has gone beyond the practical possibilities.

WHY ARE FORECASTS MADE?

Population forecasts made 15 years ago for the mid 1980s were mostly overestimates. Nearly 30% of UK school places lie empty for example. What is the relevance of techniques of population forecasting to the complicated interactions of social, economic, medical and other factors influencing the position of women (and men) in society and all the other influences on the number of children born?

Some authors claim that the consequences are not serious even if forecasts are wrong (Martin 1980). No doubt some land uses can respond. Others such as schools certainly can not. Even when forecasts go wrong at least the activity of forecasting gives early warning of this. Also, for some development particularly shopping, there are good commercial reasons for forecasting.

Also accuracy is not necessarily the only aim of forecasting. For some phenomena such as environmental pollution, the purpose of a forecast may be to be self-defeating. The 'scare' value of a forecast may help cause action to prevent it coming to be.

METHODS OF FORECASTING POPULATION

Generally, methods of forecasting are based on extrapolation of trends modified by the effects of occurrences which are thought likely to take place. Extrapolation of trends can take any of several forms. It may be assumed that the total population of an area for example, changes as a proportion of that at the most reliable survey:

$$P_f = P_i C$$

where P_i is the initial population at the last count
P_f is the population at the forecast date
C is a constant calculated by fitting to past trends

Less commonly, population may be assumed to change by a constant amount:

$$P_f = P_i + C \quad \text{or} \quad P_f = P_i + C_{f-i}$$

In fact, many formulae can be derived using for example logarithms of population against time or against logarithm of time. The choice is to a large extent dependent on what best fits past trends. Several examples of formulae and the testing of them for accuracy are explained in Isserman (1977).

In situations where forecasts have been made for a large population, forecasts for a part of that population may be made by what have been termed ratio projections. For example

$$P_f = \frac{P_i \times L_f}{L_i}$$

where L_f is the larger population at the forecast date
L_i is the larger population at the last accurate count

so that for example

forecast number of persons over 60 in Town X	=	Total population Town X	x	forecast number of persons over 60 in Region Y
		Total population Region Y		

This formula assumes a constant ratio between larger and smaller populations. Alternatively, it may be found that a variable ratio fits past trends more closely:

$$P_f = C \frac{P_i \cdot L_f}{L_i}$$

These kinds of formulae are likely to be most accurate where none of the populations is small (as they can easily be influenced by relatively small disturbing influences such as the building of an old persons home or a housing scheme) and for relatively stable age groups. Those most likely to migrate are likely to cause these projections to be inaccurate, and so too are children as birth rates are notoriously difficult to predict.

Population forecasting at the scale of the county

At all but a local scale, the cohort survival method is one of the most common and most accurate methods of population projection. This consists of separate projections for males and females. Each sex is divided into age groups at a time when a reliable enumeration has taken place such as a Census. Five year age groups are the usual compromise. Smaller groups increase data handling resources necessary whilst there is is loss of accuracy for large age categories. Death rates are applied to each age group to calculate the number expected to survive to the year of the forecast (five years into the future in table 6.1). When available, these death rates should be specifically for the local area and a recent year. Death rates vary quite considerably between one part of the country and another and a little through time. There is also a very large difference in death rates between males and females and it is very important not to apply an average rate.

For the female age groups of child bearing age, birth rates are also applied to estimate the number in the 0-4 category for the forecast date. A mortality rate must be applied to these children as some will both be born and die within the period of the forecast. The estimation of death rate raises some problems. Some of the children will be born towards the end of the forecast period and there will clearly be less chance of them dying than those born earlier in the period. The rate is likely to be less than that for the 0-4 age group of those already born at the Census date. If we reason that the children are born at an approximately equal rate throughout the five year period it might lead us to expect this death rate to be half that of the previous 0-4 age group. The death rate in the first year is much higher than for 1-4 year olds (9.5 and 0.3 per thousand respectively for the East Midlands in 1982 (OPCS 1984)). In Table 6.1, the mortality rate was calculated by applying the first year death rate (9.5 per thousand) and 3.5 times the 1-4 year death rate of 0.3 per thousand for those born within the first year of the Census. For the second year after the Census it was 9.5 plus 2.5 times 0.3 and so on up to the children born within the year prior to the forecast date. Another problem with this figure is of course, that the death rate itself has been projected. It has

59

Table 6.1
Cohort Survival Method of Population Projection
applied to Leicestershire

AGE	FEMALES 1981	5-YEAR DEATH RATE PER 1,000	SURVIVAL TO 1986	ANNUAL BIRTH RATE PER 1,000
0-4	26,326	10	27,095	
5-9	28,669		26,063	
10-14	33,656	1	28,640	
15-19	34,299		33,622	28
20-24	30,878		34,265	102
25-29	29,364	3	30,847	126
30-34	32,663		29,276	69
35-39	27,193	5	32,565	22
40-44	23,585		27,057	5
45-49	22,604	17	23,467	
50-54	23,331		22,220	
55-59	23,725	49	22,934	
60-64	20,348		22,562	
65-69	20,371	114	19,351	
70-74	18,196		18,049	
75-79	14,091	293	16,122	
80-84	8,907		9,962	
85+	6,002	631	8,512	

Sources of information: OPCS (1981), (1982a), (1982b), (1982c),
(1984), Central Statistical Office (1984).

Table 6.1
continued

CHILDREN BORN		DEATH RATE		SURVIVORS	
51.3%	48.7%				
MALES	FEMALES	MALES	FEMALES	MALES	FEMALES
28,714	27,259	6	6	28,542	27,095

been assumed constant, though this is not a serious source of error over short periods.

Death rates may be applied to male age groups to estimate the number of survivors to the forecast date. Together with the female table, this will give an estimate of population excluding migration, and this is perhaps the most complicated problem to overcome.

Migration estimates based on past trends are unsatisfactory because unlike death rates, migration is liable to change over a short period of time. It is much more accurate to enquire into the causes of migration as a basis for estimation. Causes at the scale of a county might include proposals for job creation or redundancy and plans for building. The problems are two-fold. Firstly, there is the problem of estimating how many jobs or how much building is involved. Secondly, there is the even more difficult problem of estimating the effects on population movement. This can only be done by survey of effects in the recent past. These and some other problems are deriving migration rates are discussed in OPCS (1980).

This case shows some of the weaknesses of the cohort survival technique. The five year death rates were calculated by raising the annual death rates to the power of 5. They were treated as probabilities of dying in each year. However, as time passes, an increasing number of each age group pass to the next older age group. The question of which death rate to apply becomes ambiguous. This may account for the calculated increase in population over 75. The annual birth rates were multiplied by 5 to calculate the 5-year rate on the assumption that the same woman can give birth more than once in the 5-year period.

Often, it is more reliable to estimate the future number of households rather than population. The principles behind the cohort survival method can be used for this purpose. Household projections have varied in methodology used. Useful discussions are contained in Pope (1972), Cheshire County Council (1976) and Essex County Council (1979). Basically such methods consist of:

1. Prediction of future number of dwellings from the initial stock, commitments to build and other estimated development and estimates of demolitions.

2. Division of initial households into cohorts or groups based on period since formation, often disaggregated by

tenure.

3. Estimation of dispersal or disappearance rates for households resulting from emigration, death or joining together.

4. Estimation of rates of formation of new households from population characteristics and building rates.

5. Calculation of future number of households. Future number of people by broad age groups, for example pre-school, working, retired are usually estimated for the predicted number of households. These estimates depend on there being a relationship between the period since household formation and the age characteristics of those within the households. Checks can be made by survey.

Migrants usually differ in age structure from the initial resident population. They often contain a disproportionately high number of the young adult age groups, perhaps aged 20 - 40, with young children. In some towns, particularly seaside resorts, there may be a high proportion in the older age groups. These factors may have a considerable influence on birth and death rates and may cause some adjustment to the rates used to be necessary.

The cohort survival method is therefore a form of trend projection but disaggregated by age and sex. The trends which are projected more closely describe the study area than the kind of trend projection which simply examines trends in total population. It is however, only a starting point in population forecasting. The effects of migration can radically affect the outcome and it is quite unsatisfactory to project these as trends.

Population forecasting at a local scale

Migration is the main problem for the cohort survival method. The method is a good starting point for population forecasts for study areas where movements are small in relation to the total number of inhabitants. This tends to be the case in larger study areas simply because many local movements would be confined entirely within them and because in large areas there is a better chance of in- and out-migration cancelling each other out.

Population forecasting for districts of cities, small towns or rural areas for example, may be just as important in planning services such as schools as they are at the county level. At this local scale, future population totals are greatly affected by quite small numbers of out-migrants caused by closure of a place of employment for example, or in-migration resulting from building development. The cohort survival method is therefore less accurate for these small areas. It may be used as a starting point to predict changes in the existing population but more attention will be given to changes resulting from physical development, economic and social factors.

Also, at a local scale, the influence of planning itself on future population and other characteristics becomes more evident. Even a single large planned development can reverse a population trend. Cuthbertson, Foreman-Peck and Gripaios (1982) have examined the effects of local authority spending on population in urban areas and have found that increased expenditure significantly increases population, especially when not accompanied by proportionate rate rises.

The problems of forecasting in local planning are therefore even greater than for larger populations. Migration is proportionately greater and so too are changes in the amount and occupancy of housing or other development. Planning itself has proportionately greater influence. Perhaps it is for these reasons that quantitative forecasting has not been so prominent in local plans compared with county structure plans for example. Nevertheless, for some purposes such as planning for schools, forecasting is necessary, albeit hazardous; see Morgan and Rudzitis (1978).

For many kinds of local forecasting, physical change, such as in the number of houses, is the starting point. Estimates are then made of changes in occupancy of existing and new buildings. The first step - estimating changes in the number of dwellings - is much easier than the second. In an inner city district such as Small Heath in Birmingham for example, physical changes could be estimated by reference to:

- City Council and housing association intentions for development and the effects of Central Government fiscal policies upon them.

- vacant land designated for housing by the City Council as local planning authority and an estimate of the way this is likely to be taken up by the private sector. This will be influenced by such factors as local house prices, land costs and agreements under section 52 of the Town and Country Planning Act 1971, whereby developers can be encouraged to develop unattractive sites as a condition of being granted profitable planning permissions elsewhere.

Estimating physical change is problematical but not so much so as estimating future usage of the physical development expected to be present. Many planners working locally have related physical development to usage, such as estimates of the number of dwellings to the number of residents, or office floorspace to jobs created. Generally, these estimates have varied a lot according to place and from time to time. Some estimates for industrial floorspace and jobs are reviewed in Stone (1973). Many local authorities have carried out similar surveys for housing and residents with results very different from each other. It is common to predict the number of children and school requirements from factors such as house tenure, floor area, number of rooms, number of storeys and car spaces.

As a general rule it has been found that newly built housing passes through several stages in terms of its occupiers. At first there is usually a high proportion of young couples and during the first decade the number of children increases. Afterwards the total population often remains fairly stable or declines slowly as children grow up and move out. After perhaps a couple of decades this decrease accelerates and the proportion of adults and later old people, increases. Sometimes those who grew up in the estate as children move to set up home nearby and with their own children, increasing the need for facilities such as schools. Meanwhile the schools once attended by these parents are left with spare places. This general course of events has been quite common in new towns. After another decade or more, the proportion of old people declines as they die and are replaced by younger families.

Such a picture of population changes may give some guidance as to what to expect and what kind of surveys will be necessary. It can, however, be greatly distorted according to the sizes, prices and form of dwellings and their location. Events could be very different at the seaside where there may be an influx of retired people. House prices may have some effect on family size whilst so too could incomes locally and availability of finance. Decisions by families on where to live are also influenced by the availability of the facilities being planned and influenced by the forecasts. Perceived quality and location of schools are important to many parents. Obviously there is some movement according to the change in composition of the family. This and the reasons for household relocation are examined in Clark and Onaka (1983) and Robertson (1982).

All of these factors tend to confuse relationships between forecasts of dwellings and forecasts of residents. These factors often apply in specific ways locally, and this is no doubt part of the explanation as to why any relationships between the number and kind of dwellings and residents are at best, reliable only locally.

Estimates which relate population characteristics to housing characteristics may be carried out in two basic ways. Firstly changes through time can be observed in selected housing. This may seem the obvious way to approach the task but there are problems. The boundaries of statistical units such as census enumeration districts change from time to time. Statistical units often contain several house types and the required data can not be separated out. Perhaps most serious however, is that there will be external influences on the population changes which are independent of the nature of the housing. Changes in family size due to economic or social changes have been taking place continuously. To some extent the local effects of these factors can be filtered out by comparing local and regional or national trends in occupancy.

A second and more common way of relating population to housing characteristics is to compare housing of different ages at one time. The problems of the first approach are replaced by the problems of selecting housing which is truly comparable in every way other than age. Linear regression is quite commonly used in the following general form:

$$Y_j = a + b_1 X_{1j} + b_2 X_{2j} \cdots b_n X_{nj}$$

where Y_j is one of the dependent variables, for example the population in a specified age group

X_{ij} is an independent variable, the number of dwellings in catchment area j of the type i for example 5-roomed council houses

a is a constant

b is a coefficient produced by the regression equation

To estimate the number of children aged 5 to 10 for example, this would be regarded as the dependent variable Y_j. The factors expected to affect the number of children of this age in a specified housing area are then enumerated as the independent variables. These might include the number of bedrooms and number of houses built within the previous 15 years for example. Using a computer package such as the Statistical Package for the Social Sciences it is possible to find out which independent variable has the most influence on

66

the dependent variable. Other independent variables can then be examined to find out how far they influence the dependent variable. Regression equations can be produced for each step. For the Vale Royal district of Cheshire, Thomas and Moorcroft (1977) developed such a method for estimating total population, age groups and client groups such as library users and relating these to the tenure, size and age of housing.

These forecasting methods for population do not need much adaption for other kinds of forecasting.

SOME ISSUES IN FORECASTING EMPLOYMENT AND FUTURE LAND USES

Particularly in large study areas, larger than may be covered by a local plan and where some degree of self containment between related industries and other employment activities occurs, it will be desirable to forecast basic and non basic (dependent) employment separately. This will be even more important if the forecast is to cover a sufficient period of time that a significant amount of new employment sources may become established. If the forecast is for more than a few years, new service industries may be attracted to any imbalance of basic industries, services which cannot be foretold from a survey of existing firms. And so, the decision of whether or not to divide existing sources of employment into basic and dependent sectors often depends on whether or not a survey of existing firms to enquire of their intentions will be adequate. Is the study area so large that new firms could be attracted whose employment could not be adequately predicted? Is the period of time of the forecast so long that employers' intentions are likely to be less reliable than trend forecasts?

Basic (exporting) industries are those which contribute to the exportable commodities or services of the study area and which thereby generate earnings from outside. These earnings are partly used for paying for essential services from dependent activities such as builders and property repairers, retail activities, school teachers and in fact most government employees. The ratio between basic employment and dependent employment is the multiplier for each type of activity. It will be evident that the distinction between basic and dependent employment is far from clear. Some activities can be both, for example baking: which category activities fall into depends on the size of the study area.

Usually such projections are made for the sub-region or region but there is no reason why the distinction could not be made for forecasting employment for a reasonably self-contained town.

Where there is doubt as to whether a given industry is basic or non-basic, calculating indices such as the location quotient may be helpful:

$$\text{Location quotient} = \frac{\text{No. of employees in a given industry in area X/Total employees in area X}}{\text{No. of employees in the same industry in area Y/Total employees in area Y}}$$

If the study area was area X and perhaps England and Wales area Y, then location quotient would give an indication of the degree of concentration of the given industry. If this was significantly greater than unity there would be some grounds for assuming the industry to be basic.

Basic employment may be foretold by assuming national, regional or local change rates and applying these to the existing situation in the same way as trend forecasts are made in population and household forecasting.

Forecasts of non-basic employment may be made by using assumptions about the rate of basic/non-basic employment taking advantage of research such as that relating to the Social Accounting Matrix prepared by the Department of Applied Economics at Cambridge University. Information on past employment trends is also often available from the Department of Employment, the National Economic Development Council and the National Institute for Economic and Social Research.

Input-output analysis is a useful method of laying out the effects of changes in production in one sector or others and therefore the effects of changes in employment.

	Industry			Households
	x	y	z	
Industry X	17	38	56	43
Industry Y	27	21	4	25
Industry Z	11	9	29	20
Households	45	32	11	10

In the above table the rows represent inputs the columns outputs and the figures are £ million. Thus £100 million output from industry Y is made up as follows: £38 million from industry X, £21 million from Y, £9 million from Z and £32 million from households (largely labour). If expansion in industry Y takes place there will be similar increases in the other industries. The effects of these expansions can then be calculated as a 'second round'. The process can be repeated until the expansions are negligible. For a fuller explanation of the technique see Isard (1960) or Masser (1972).

In forecasting employment for very large areas where the effects of immigration may not be significant, analysis may be made of population characteristics as an aid to forecasting the labour force. For example, a number of population trends are frequently assumed relevant to forecasting labour force:

a) birth rate in past affecting the number of new workers and the numbers retiring,

b) attractiveness of work to married women - changes in birth rate, equal pay, job opportunities,

c) numbers in full-time education,

d) fall in numbers working beyond retiring age.

Forecasts may be made on the basis of extrapolation of these trends. The main drawbacks of such forecasts are their lack of sensitivity to changes in economic activity and demand for jobs.

In smaller study areas, perhaps in towns of up to 80,000 - 100,000 population, and especially when the period of the forecast is short and where the amount of new land available for employment uses is small, forecasts made by questionnaire survey of developers intentions will sometimes be more accurate. Projections based on assumed rates of change can be upset by abnormal behaviour from a single large employer. At the regional scale these tend to cancel each other out, but locally, surveys of employers' intentions will often be essential to forecasting.

Even so, there are many hazards in forecasting:

- changes in demand for products or services
- changes in taxation and subsidies

- technological changes - substitution of capital for
  labour, wage changes
- availability of finance for expansion
- availability of land and permission for expansion - e.g.
  planning permission.

The list of unknowns facing an employer when asked to state
his future intentions is almost endless. Useful reviews of
local employment forecasting are Hunt et al (1980) and Danson
et al (1980).

So far we have been concerned with forecasting the number of
jobs by sector of employment or by type of occupation e.g.
professional, skilled manual, unskilled manual. The two main
methods relying on assumed trends or rates of change and
surveys of employees intentions coupled with commitment such
as zoning and outstanding planning permissions are both
extremely hazardous. Both methods may be used together;
otherwise choice between them depends on the size and nature
of study area (large areas with large amounts of new land
available tend to favour trend forecasts) and the period of
time of the forecast.

Sometimes forecasting the future number of jobs will be
sufficient - particularly in cases where there is little new
land available. Forecasts of the number and type of jobs may
be used to provide evidence and formulate policies for
applications for planning permission likely to result in
changes in employment, for example the change from
manufacturing industry to warehousing, which usually results
in a loss of employment. In some studies however, it will be
required to forecast the demand for land for employers as well
as the number of jobs.

The principles of forecasting land use needs for employers
are as simple as forecasting the number and type of jobs - and
equally hazardous. There are two essential steps:

1) Land uses for employers are not entirely interchangeable.
Offices and manufacturing industry for example usually require
different sites. A first step is therefore to decide what
categories of land use are required so that (a) all employers'
requirements will fall within one category (b) any of the land
within one category can be used by all employers whose
requirement fall into it.

In the South Hampshire study, four categories were used
(Kirkbride 1970):

detached offices, i.e. offices not sharing a site with related activities such as manufacturing industry

attached offices e.g. factory offices

manufacturing industry

others e.g. agriculture, construction, warehousing, transport, education

A more detailed classification may be necessary at a local scale. It is certainly likely that the last two categories would be sub-divided in local planning. Manufacturing industry could be sub-divided according to several criteria for example:

A) Light industry as could be accommodated in a residential area, and noxious industry. The latter could be further sub-divided according to special site requirements e.g. relating to distance or direction of prevailing winds in relation to the built up area.

B) Local requirements, e.g. transport, skilled labour supply.

2) Relate the forecasts for the number of jobs in each land use category to assumed intensities of employment to forecast land requirements for each land use category. Figures for the number of employees per unit area of land for future dates are usually likely to be very inaccurate. Most surveys of existing firms to relate area to employment show great variations between firms even in very similar types of work.

Some surveys are reported in Stone (1973). Tempest (1982) in a study of 26 towns, counties and parts of counties found an average of 33.5 m^2 per employee (range 11.6 m^2 to 59.5 m^2) in manufacturing industry and 51.1 m^2 per employee (range 16.1 m^2 to 89.5 m^2) in warehousing. A survey of employment densities in the West Midlands (West Midlands County Council 1977) revealed an average industrial density of 82 workers per hectare varying from 20 for mining and quarrying and utilities, 47 for metal manufacture, 59 for warehousing, 89 for non-metal using manufacturing, 109 for construction to 131 for metal using manufacturing. There were very large variations between individual firms within these averages.

THE GRAVITY MODEL

The methods of forecasting so far are for resident population and job locations. It may be at least as important to forecast the number of people making journies to a particular area and the effects they might have there. For these purposes, the gravity model may be used.

Sir Isaac Newton in his Law of Universal Gravitation stated that:

> Two bodies in the universe attract each other in proportion to the product of their masses, and inversely to the square of their distances apart.

This has been translated into planning terms by substituting 'interaction' for the gravitational attraction of two bodies, 'size' or 'attractiveness' for mass. Also it has not always been assumed that it is the <u>square</u> of the distance apart that explains attraction. In its simplest form, the gravity model may therefore be represented as:

$$T_{ij} = K \ (A_i A_j)/d_{ij}^{\ c})$$

where T_{ij} = number of trips by residents of zone i to zone j
$A_i A_j$ = size of zones i and j
d_{ij} = distance between zones i and j
c = an exponent (not necessarily 2 as would follow from Newton)
K = a constant which is calculated to fit actual conditions.

Richardson (1969) p.100 argues for the application of exponents A to take into account agglomeration economies (exponent > 1) and diseconomies of scale for example due to congestion (exponent < 1). If agglomeration economies were due to scale the exponent would vary according to the size of A.

This equation represents only the interaction between two zones, i and j. Sometimes it is useful to work out the relationship between one zone and all other zones for which the equation may be modified to become

$$\sum_{j=1}^{n} T_{ij} = K \sum_{j=1}^{n} \frac{A_i A_j}{d_{ij}{}^c}$$

This simple form of the model does not take into account the relative attraction of competing zones. Lee (1973) compensates for this by introducing a balancing factor into the denominator:

$$T_{ij} = \frac{\dfrac{G\, P_i P_j}{d_{ij}{}^c}}{G\, \dfrac{P_1}{d_{i1}{}^c} + G\, \dfrac{P_2}{d_{i2}{}^c} + G\, \dfrac{P_3}{d_{i3}{}^c} + \ldots G\, \dfrac{P_n}{d_{in}{}^c}}$$

Re-writing and cancelling G, this becomes

$$T_{ij} = \frac{P_i P_j\, d_{ij}{}^{-c}}{\displaystyle\sum_{j=1}^{n} P_j\, d_{ij}{}^{-c}}$$

The units for A depend on the subject of the application, two of the most common being journey to work and shopping patterns. For journey to work it has often been population sometimes weighted by income or type of occupation. For shopping, area of retailing, number of shops, scales, numbers employed or rateable value may be used for example.

Distance may be measured as the shortest route, travelling time or transport costs. Often different measures will be necessary for different modes of transport, i.e. applying one distance for one mode and another distance for another mode.

Planning for shopping with the Gravity Model

Shopping models can have any of several purposes:

- to forecast the amount of floorspace needed in future
- to estimate needs for change in overall shopping provision
- to indicate needs for traffic management measures and

public transport (may also be used to estimate latent potential demand due to the price structure)
- to indicate whether shopping should be combined with other uses such as offices, recreation or social facilities.

Applying the gravity model comprises six essential steps:

1) Definition of the study area. If the purpose is to estimate the required size of the proposed new shopping centre then its estimated catchment area would be used.

2) Division of the study area into zones. For accuracy, zones should be as small as possible within constraints set by data and resources available to analyse it.

3) Forecasts are made of population and estimated spending power (on the kinds of goods available from the new shopping centre) for each zone.

4) At this stage, it may increase accuracy to divide the goods into categories such as convenience and durable (depending on whether the shopping centre will provide both and whether the catchment areas for each are likely to be significantly different). Stages 5 and 6 will be carried out separately for each category of goods.

5) Identification of competing shopping centres.

6) Application of the gravity formulae. There are many formulae in use but generally they include the following basic elements:

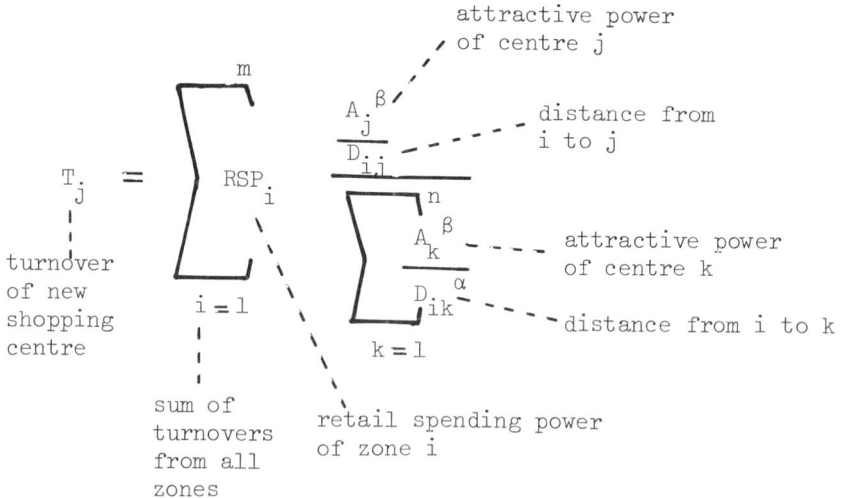

74

See for example Murray and Kennedy (1971).

Example: Zone i has a total spending power of £8m per year on goods available at a proposed shopping parade. This parade will have a retail sales area of 100,000 m^2 and will be 10 minutes from the centre of zone i. There is only one other shopping centre serving zone i. This is centre k with 200,000 m^2 sales area and 40 minutes from zone i. How much will be spent by zone i residents at the new shopping parade?

$$Tj = £8m \times \dfrac{\dfrac{100{,}000}{10}}{\dfrac{100{,}000}{10} + \dfrac{200{,}000}{40}}$$

= £5.333m per year

notes:

- attractive powers of the new shopping parade and centre k could have been measured in any of several ways other than retail floor area, for example rateable value, turnover or number of employees.

- the exponents a and b were assumed to be 1. Often, these may be calculated when Tj is known - the model is calibrated - and then are applied to the formula for a period when Tj is not known.

- if the total turnover of the new shopping parade is required, the same procedure should be repeated for all zones within the catchment area.

Problems of applying gravity models

1 There is no reasoned explanation of why they should explain interaction. It is a reasonable assumption that interactions depend on the attractiveness of zones and vary inversely with distance, as accounted for in gravity models. But it is also reasonable that the extent of interactions depend on many other factors as well - the constraints on land availability applied by ownership and the need for planning permission, positive direction of development by zoning and the availability of finance and land for communications to mention only a few factors. Also there is no reason to assume that the variables are

related to each other in any particular way. Common sense leads us to expect that the effect of distance on interaction is not uniform, longer distances being even more of a deterrent that would otherwise be expected. There are obvious limits to which any shoppers will travel. Equally there is no good reason why the exponent should be constant between all pairs of zones or between journeys for different purposes. This problem of journeys for different purposes can be alleviated by disaggregating the models but only at the expense of losing the predictability of large group behaviour and by greatly increasing data requirements.

2. Calibration. Batty (1970) points out the danger of fitting the constants and exponents so that predicted and actual interactions are similar. Although the total number of journeys will be represented by the model, the reasons for them are unexplained. This is very significant when we remember how the planning implications differ between journeys to work, shops and entertainment for example. In other words, gravity models tend to provide a better description of interaction than an explanation.

3. Gravity models are based on retrospective relationships and are static.

4. Calculations are based on averages.

5. They assume perfect knowledge and rationality of the subjects.

6. Disadvantages of central locations, for example car parking and congestion, tend to make some models inaccurate.

7. The arbitrariness of definition of zones. Often, large zones are necessary to obtain reasonably accurate information - for forecasting population and other variables - and there is a conflict with the need for small zones in order that the centroids may be representative. The boundaries of zones are often somewhat arbitrary, groups of census enumeration districts or wards being common. And yet these are clearly very significant in applying any spatial model. Also boundaries are sharply defined in the application of models whereas in practice they are more likely to be zones rather than lines.

8. Shopping models ignore price competition between shops and the effects of age and sex composition on shopping habits.

These problems are certainly liable to be serious. Some of them can be alleviated at the expense of making the model more complicated, laborious and demanding of data. As for most planning techniques, it is a question of selecting the right situation to apply the gravity model and being able to put the results into perspective. The reliability of shopping models is reviewed in Turner and Cole (1980).

7 Approaches to plan preparation

Most approaches to plan or policy preparation ultimately amount to either solving problems or realising opportunities - a glance at the objectives of most planning studies will reveal that they can be put into one or other of these categories.   Indeed, solving problems and realising opportunities are a starting point for preparing a plan.   In a constrained urban situation, planners will probably be pressed firstly into problem solving, though even here it would be a very one-sided kind of plan which did not even look to bringing into use whatever opportunities there might be.   At the other extreme in a new town, initial constraints may be few, and although a purpose of the new town may be to solve a problem elsewhere, there may be few local problems which planners would be called upon to solve.   With a blank sheet to start with, they will be able to consider the possibility of whole neighbourhood or even whole town design - which configuration of land uses would be most efficient in terms of accessibility and other criteria overall?   This is not a question which would be of much concern to planners in constrained city areas as they can only affect the pattern of land uses in a minor way and only gradually.   For greenfield sites therefore, there is the possibility of whole town design using models of settlement patterns or stereotypes as they are sometimes called.   Most New Town Plans give some consideration to this approach - so too have some sub-regional studies (see for example Kozlowski 1968).

At one extreme in a constrained urban area therefore, planners might start with a list of problems that they hope to alleviate. At the other extreme, new town planners may regard their prime job as one of planning settlements for convenience, efficiency and prosperity so as to avoid the kind of problems facing urban areas. These are two approaches. Somewhat in between is the situation of plans for the expansion of an existing town. There are constraints and problems to be solved - there may also be opportunities such as spare capacity in infrastructure to serve some sites. There are several techniques such as threshold analysis for just this kind of job and the use of such methods of land analysis may be regarded as a third approach.

This is only one view of approaches to plan preparation. Barras and Broadbent (1979) identified two quite clear approaches to generation in early structure plans in addition to those based on model settlements or 'design concepts'. Firstly there were strategies related to land supply and secondly those based on "development potential".

Bracken (1981 Ch 2) distinguishes two approaches to plan generation:

1) The "systematic development of the traditional design process in urban planning". This involves analysis of problem structure and he indicates two approaches to this:
A) land analysis e.g. by development potential surface analysis
B) Markov theory. This depends on tracing the relationships between the problems within an area. By solving the more detailed problems e.g. car parking within a large shopping centre, and generally passing on to the more fundamental one, these are eventually tackled. Problem solving takes place by tracing the attitudes of those involved and compromise. This is a useful method of explaining a problem but is less useful as a way of solving it.

2) The strategic choice approach. An attempt is made to trace all the alternatives (land use, timing, type of developer, building form etc.), uncertainties and possible courses of action. By ruling out the combinations which are not possible, the choices for the decision maker are made much clearer. AIDA uses many of these principles (see below, Friend and Jessop (1976) and Openshaw and Whitehead (1978)). Structure plans which have used these principles include 'Strategic Choice for East Anglia'

(1974) DoE, and West Berkshire (Bather et al 1975).

One possible criticism of the kinds of approach mentioned so far is that they rely too much on the mechanical application of a series of procedures. They do not allow for the full range of possibilities and do not allow for innovation. One kind of attempt to overcome this which has been used on a few occasions is the Delphi technique and scenario writing which may take place together or separately. (See the special issue of The Planner for April 1974 on Futurology). The Delphi technique starts out with the selection of a group of experts who are asked to select issues and factors affecting them which they consider will be important in future. They are then asked how they see planning should shape the future at a series of given dates. The results are analysed statistically, testing for scatter and significance for example. Really, such an approach is little more than a formalisation of what might otherwise have been left to chance but perhaps this explicit reference to professional and other opinion is worthwhile.

Scenario writing may follow the Delphi technique. It is very explicitly related to alternative factors. Possible changes in attitudes and values such as towards conservation, changes in relative prices e.g. of energy and other fundamental changes are, as far as possible, made explicit. These may then be related to possible shifts in fundamental attitudes within society - for example towards a more competitive society, co-operative or humanised society, emphasising individuality and variety of choice, towards totalitarianism or conservation. There is a danger that in using this approach to escape the straight jacket of mechanical procedural planning, a lot of time and effort may be wasted on rather far-fetched ideas. Much depends on how these ideas are translated into alternative features or scenarios - the next stage. Possible future changes are related to the institutional and physical context - development commitments and constraints, physical land features, possible roles of the electorate, professionals and politicians, the extent of planning intervention, land policy e.g. towards planning gain, and the future roles of existing institutions. A series of alternative futures as affected by collections of these factors are then formulated and usually put forward for public comment. The possibilities of scenario writing in structure planning are discussed in Thornley (1977).

In many urban areas, the need for remedial planning will make this approach first choice. Needham (1971) argues a case for planners generally trying to solve problems rather than achieve goals. This would need a rather wide definition of what constitutes a problem if we are to include for example, the selection of sites involving lowest construction cost. However, a glance at the objectives of most recent structure plans and local plans will reveal the extent to which planning is a problem solving, remedial activity as well as an objective chasing task.

A useful way of setting out the problems of an area is the Analysis of Interconnected Decision Areas (AIDA); see Hickling (1974 and 1978). AIDA is a useful way of laying out clearly the options, constraints and opportunities that face decision-makers. It is very much a method of laying out systematically what is already known rather than a way of finding out new facts. It can be applied to many questions in planning, for example choice of land use for a given site, choice between several sites for an intended use, alternative densities, choice between levels of investment in public transport.

Applying the analysis of interconnected decision areas in land use allocations

1) **Definition of decision areas.** Decision areas are the fields in which there is a choice between alternatives. To identify and define them we need to know what factors influence the subject being studied (land use in this case). A possible decision area not included, is that of tenure - housing or industry for rent or sale? This was left out largely because it is a question which could be considered separately afterwards (Table 7.1).

2) **Definition of alternatives within each decision area.** Let use assume nine alternative sites. In practice definition of these will result from land potential studies which must preceed AIDA.

3) **Construction of options compatibility matrix.** Each pair of alternatives is then checked for compatibility using information from land potential studies. The results are entered in the form of a matrix table (Table 7.1).

In AIDA there is no indication of degrees of compatibility or costs or benefits from alternatives. As Hickling suggests (Hickling 1978), these could be kept as separate records.

Table 7.1

An Options Compatibility Matrix

	SITES 1	2	3	4	5	6	7	8	9	USE 1	2	3	DENSITY 1	2	3	TIMING 1	2	3	AGENCY 1	2	3
USE 1	*	*		*	*	*	*														
USE 2					*	*	*	*	*												
USE 3									*		*										
DENSITY 1		*	*	*																	
DENSITY 2				*		*	*							*	*						
DENSITY 3			*											*	*						
TIMING 1	*	*																			
TIMING 2		*																			
TIMING 3			*																		
AGENCY 1	*	*			*	*	*				*			*							
AGENCY 2	*	*			*	*	*				*	*			*						
AGENCY 3			*	*		*	*										*			*	*
SITES 1																					
SITES 2																					
SITES 3																					
SITES 4																					
SITES 5																					
SITES 6																					
SITES 7																					
SITES 8																					
SITES 9																					

Notes to Table 7.1

Decision areas are arranged as far as possible in
the order in which decisions are likely to be taken.
The compatibility of site against site is decided last
because only after density and timing have been
considered will it be known whether or not all sites
will be needed.

* means that the options are incompatible

USE   1   housing
          2   industry
          3   open space

DENSITY   1   housing 30+ per hectare
               industry 2,500m^2+ per hactare
          2   housing 20-29 per hectare
               industry 1,500-2,499m^2 per hactare
          3   housing less than 20 per hactare
               industry less than 1,500m^2 per hactare

TIMING   1   within 5 years
          2   5-10 years
          3   more than 10 years

AGENCY   1   local authority
          2   housing association
          3   private

use   density   time

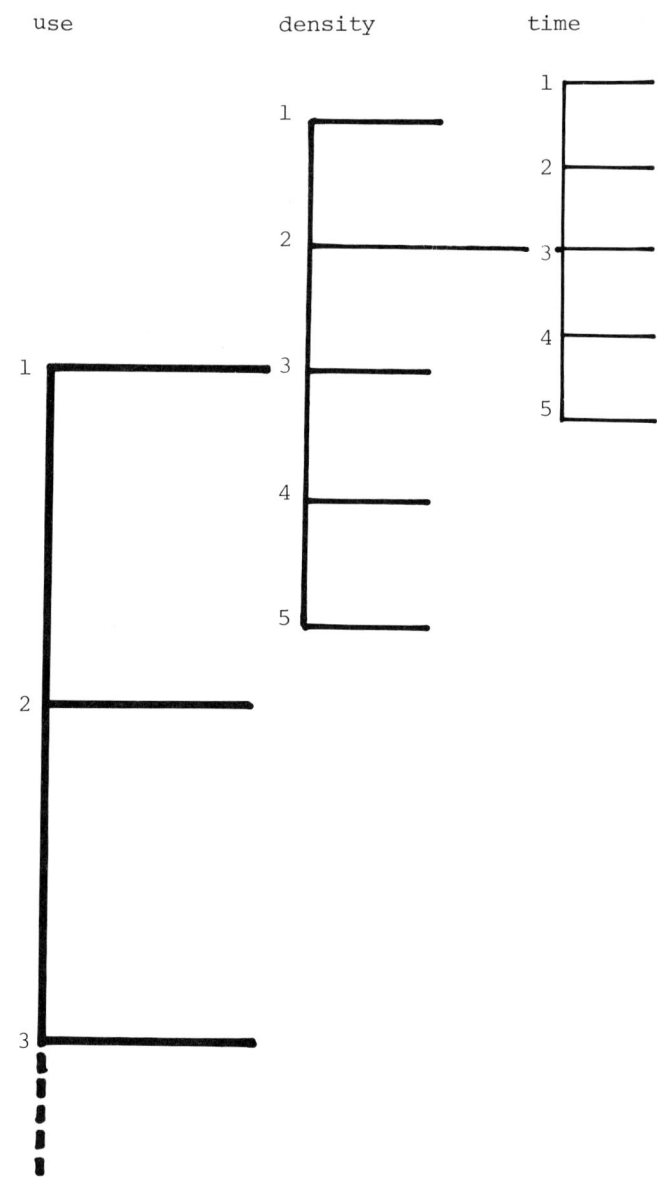

Figure 7.1 Part of a solution tree

84

They would, however, involve a large input of information and there would not be much indication of which relationships require the greatest accuracy. In short, there are a very large number of combinations of alternatives and there is a danger of wasting a great deal of labour and information resources.

4) <u>Identification of alternative courses of action</u>. Where there are a relatively small number of alternatives, it is possible to plot these by means of what has sometimes been called a solution tree (Figure 7.1).

It will be clear that when all uses, density, timings and agencies are considered that a very large number of combinations will result.

<u>The uses and limitations of AIDA.</u>

Uses

- It provides a systematic framework for laying out a great deal of information that has already been collected and for indentifying gaps in information.

- AIDA is a very versatile technique and can be applied to a wide range of decisions other than land use allocation; for example, in policy and investment planning such as the sale of public housing or investment in transport or in the programming of development.

- Because it requires a large amount of information, it is likely to be applied in the latter part of the analysis stage and in the early part of formulating alternative schemes. It can also be used for testing alternatives by checking the feasibility of the components.

Limitations

- It only shows what is feasible, not the costs and benefits of alternatives. An important feature of many other planning techniques is their ability to eliminate unlikely alternatives quickly, thereby avoiding spending much time in accurately calculating costs and benefits. This allows concentration on the more finely balanced alternatives, where the choice is not obvious. AIDA demonstrates all conceivable possibilities but is not well adapted for concentrating effort where it really matters.

- AIDA only tells in a systematic way to the decision-maker

what he already knows. No new facts come from applying it.

- In this example, the options within each decision area were greatly simplified and reduced in number to prevent an unmanageable number of combinations. For example, to represent reality there should be several more sub-divisions in decision areas and probably several more decision areas. There is a danger that the decision area alternatives may not be sufficiently precise to be sure whether or not an option bar applies. The more alternatives within the decision areas, the more unwieldy the number of combinations becomes and the more risk there is of wasted labour and data.

MODEL SETTLEMENTS

Where there is scope to have some effect on urban structure, either where there is likely to be a large amount of development over a short period as in a new town, or in long term strategic planning, ideal settlement forms may be considered. These 'stereotypes' as they are sometimes called, are the result of considering various forms of accessibility. The physical, social and economic constraints which will be encountered when it comes to applying them to real world situations are considered separately at a later stage.

Over the centuries, many and varied settlement patterns have been proposed by social reformers and more latterly by architects and town planners. However, it seems that most are combinations of three basic principles: concentration, dispersal and linear settlements. A useful article comparing model settlement forms is Albers (1968).

Concentration

It has been the occurrence of dense urban areas under the influence of free market forces that has given rise to many problems of urban settlements. Nevertheless, limited and controlled concentration is often planned. High density inner city housing is planned to bring 'life' back, perhaps to an office or shopping area. Green belt and other policies of restriction aim at concentrating urban growth in order to conserve land or protect the landscape.

Advantages are as follows:

1) Reduces travelling distances thereby reducing time spent travelling and investment in roads, railways etc. For the

same reason, concentration also reduces investments in other infrastructure such as drainage, water supply, gas and electricity supply and the cost of operating public transport services.

2) Gives greater accessibility of residents to jobs, shops and other facilities, and therefore greater choice.

3) Reduces land taken up for urban uses.

   Disadvantages are as follows:

1) Overconcentration without suitable building forms results in lack of the facilities normally expected for a healthy existence e.g. open space. Definition of suitable building forms for high density living and what is a maximum satisfactory density are both questions of contention.

2) Urban growth is difficult because uses become hemmed in. Often this results in building becoming converted to different and often unsuited uses, or development being relatively expensive due to land acquisition or demolition costs.

Dispersal

Policies for both concentration and dispersal have long been fundamental to British planning - concentration of some cities by imposition of green belt and other policies and dispersal of overspill to new and expanded towns. Invariably awareness of the advantages of concentration is a very significant element in the local planning of overspill schemes. Ebenezer Howard's notion of garden cities is a classic example of this combination.

   Advantages are as follows:

1) Improvement in the immediate environment of the individual by giving more living space, access to open space and the countryside etc.

2) Can take advantage of low land prices away from large urban areas.

Disadvantages are as follows:

1) Diminishes job opportunities to residents and access to all the other facilities that only the 'big city' can

provide.

2) Higher costs of infrastructure. Often further provision of services is cheaper in an existing town than for the establishment of a new settlement.

Linear cities

These are founded on the assumption of the importance of transport as a deciding factor in location. Theoretically all development would be either on a major transport route or a local feeder to such a route. Models differ in their provisions for segregation of local and longer distance traffic. Usually land use segregation takes place in zones or beads along the main transport route rather than as linear zones parallel to it.

The linear city has often been interpreted as a ribbon of development along a major transport route joining two existing cities – bearing more than a slight resemblance to the ribbon development of the inter-war years which was one of the factors leading to the rise of the modern British planning system. In recent years a number of British new towns such as Runcorn have used a modified version of this principle using a ring or figure of eight for the main transport route.

Advantages are as follows:

1) Efficiency of transport – all built up areas can be near a transport route without excessive convergence of routes in central areas.

2) All built up areas can be relatively near to open countryside.

3) Linear forms are relatively easily adapted to growth, although concentration of services may require some form of nuclear expansion.

Disadvantages are as follows:

1) Lengths of journeys to work, shopping etc., will be longer than in nucleated settlements of similar area. Within a given distance from any point in a linear city there is likely to be a smaller range of associated land uses because the urban development is more dispersed.

2) Elaborate segregation of transport is necessary – otherwise local traffic will impede the remainder along

the main route.

3) The need for concentration to maintain a viable clientele for services, jobs and all other land uses attracting population will tend to cause the linear concept to break down. Public transport and especially railways also tend to cause concentration of activities around stopping points.

4) Identity of towns tends to be lost.

Compromise structures involving a linear element are also very common in current practice. In facts Albers concluded that some form of linear pattern involving a system of co-ordination or central focussing of settlements best served the requirements of growth, choice of inhabitants and individuality of elements within a settlement. Clearly the advantages of ease of transport and accommodation of growth are attractive. So too are the advantages of accessibility and choice that result from concentration and these are often the combination of desirable qualities that govern the design of model settlements.

METHODS OF LAND ANALYSIS

Sieve maps, development potential surface analysis (Forbes 1969, Wannop 1972) and threshold analysis (Kozlowski and Hughes 1972, Simpson 1977 and 1983) are all used to help find sites in situations where a substantial amount of development is thought possible. They take into account existing constraints and opportunities very explicitly and are most frequently used where there is already substantial urban development.

These methods may certainly be used to identify opportunities for development - opportunities in terms of cheapest sites due to ease of accessibility to necessary services, freedom from construction hazards and so on. Some methods may also be used to identify optimum total amounts of development within a given study area - after X units of development very high investment may be necessary as a result of the need for a new reservoir, power station or some facility requiring high capital investment. These methods can also identify problems that would arise if development took place - problems of high service costs, physical unsuitability of the terrain and even 'intangibles' such as landscape damage and intangible costs of increased traffic resulting from development.

Used in conjunction with a problem solving approach, methods of land analysis would provide a formal means of analysing some of the factors relevant to locational decisions. They would introduce an element of technical rationality into a process otherwise relying on local knowledge and 'professional judgement'.

Sieve maps

These are maps of the location and extent of the factors which are adverse to development, for example steep slopes, liability to flooding, woodland, high quality agricultural land. The land which is not affected is shown to be suitable.

They are a useful, if not essential first step in finding suitable sites. The problems are:

- there is no indication of how adverse to development are the factors mapped

- not all adverse or beneficial influences can be mapped. For example, spare capacities in infrastructure and services can not always be related to which land areas could take advantage of them.

It is these problems which are addressed in development potential surface analysis and threshold analysis.

Development potential surface analysis

This is an attempt to overcome the disadvantages of sieves in that they ignore the relative importance of the factors mapped and the extent to which each factor applies in each grid square. There are various ways of applying development potential surface analysis but they all depend on deriving A) weightings to indicate the relative importance of each factor and B) a way of weighting the effects of each factor for each grid square, for example by multiplying the factor weighting by the proportion of the grid square affected. By multiplying A by B a very rough picture of which are the best grid squares for development emerges.

Development potential surface analysis is therefore a way of using quantified data on the kinds of factors which may be mapped as sieves so as to sum together the overall effects in terms of potential for development. Theoretically it is easy to knock holes in it. The derivation of the weightings has usually of necessity been unclear and ambiguous - spurious units, disregard for marginal costs, confusion of ordinal and cardinal scales (Simpson 1975). Nevertheless, it has been a useful way of stirring up public involvement in deriving opinions on what factors affect choice of sites for urban development. It has certainly been more credible as a technique for stimulating discussion than as a quantitative technique.

Threshold analysis

Threshold analysis has been developed into an accurate method of calculating the costs of development which vary from site to site. It has most frequently been applied to site costs for housing.

Maps of the distribution of land development costs can be produced. It can therefore be used as one indication of growth potential of an expanding settlement or site for a new settlement. It gives a much more accurate and informative picture of growth costs than other techniques such as sieves and development potential surface analysis. It can be a method of testing regional or structure plan proposals locally, and helps co-ordination between the scales of plan preparation.

From maps of the distribution of development costs, a sequence of development can be arranged by listing the land parcels so as to avoid high capital investment as long as possible and to make full use of it when investment is necessary. Times for capital investment can be identified for example when new estate roads, gas, electricity, water or drainage mains or facilities such as schools are needed. When these stages of development are related to a capital investment programme and data on the need for development, a realistic time scale can be determined. Threshold analysis can therefore help to introduce budgeting at an early stage of plan preparation.

Several case studies have already been explained. See Kozlowski and Hughes (1972), Scottish Development Department (1973), and Simpson (1977) and (1983). Basically it consists firstly of using sieve maps to identify which parts of the study area would be unsuitable for development at any cost, due to such reasons as land subsidence, very steep slopes or by reason of being valuable in the present use. The remainder of the technique is to calculate the costs of developing the areas of land left over.

Next, those factors which give rise to extra costs are

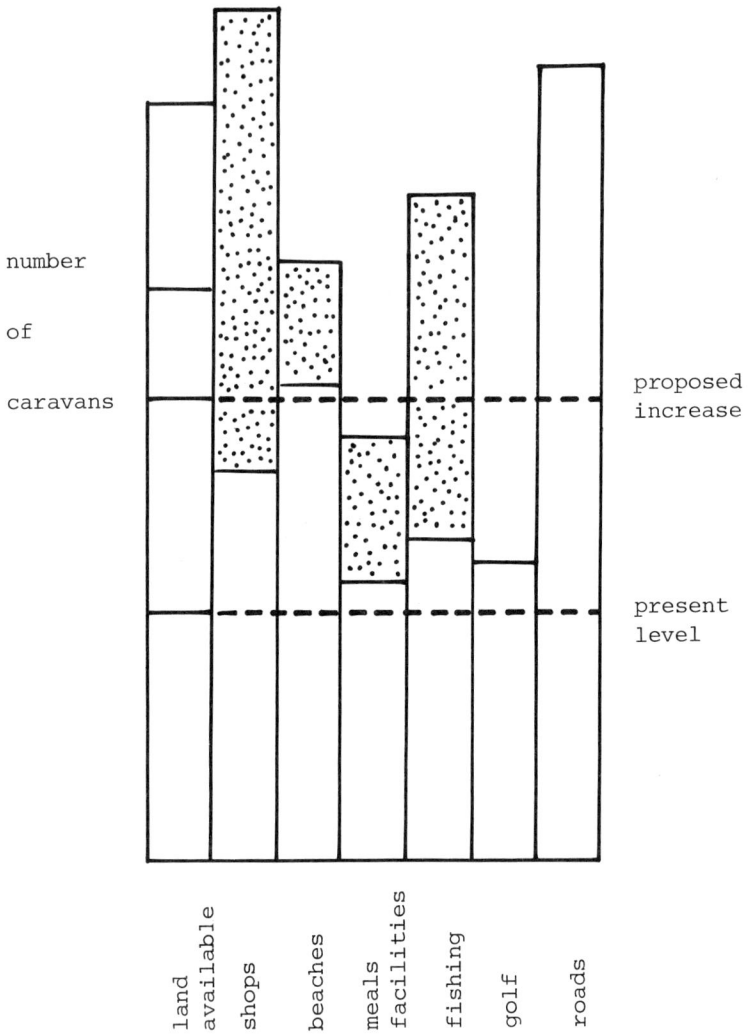

number

of

caravans

proposed
increase

present
level

land
available

shops

beaches

meals
facilities

fishing

golf

roads

Figure 7.2 Threshold analysis to show implications of
caravan parks on related facilities

mapped as far as possible. For example, a land slope of 1:10 may result in an extra cost of £900 per house, or a certain area of poor subsoil £400 per house. The maps are superimposed.

Some costs can not however be mapped in this way. Spare capacities in existing water supply, drainage, gas, electricity or in necessary facilities such as schools and health centres will be able to serve some housing within a limited radius, and will cause development of some sites to be cheaper than otherwise. To find out which sites these should be, reference is made to the maps of costs produced earlier. The sites of least cost which fall within the catchment area of services with spare capacities are those to benefit. Costs related to services can then be added to those previously calculated to give total threshold costs.

A rather different form of threshold analysis has been developed for defining tourist potential and, as part of this, environmental capacity (Kozlowski and Hughes 1972 especially chapter 7). Basically this has involved making an inventory of the resources needed for tourism: tourist attractions such as beautiful landscape, possibilities for hiking or swimming, tourist services such as hotels, restaurants, car services and other infrastructure and the labour force in tourism. The capacities and possibilites of expansion of each are then explored and limited (thresholds) determined. An example is illustrated in Figure 7.2.

Later studies (Kozlowski 1982) have used a lot of basic ecological principles to determine the environmental capacity of recreational areas. The emphasis has been on the environmental capacity of vegetation, fauna, water and relief rather than the commercial capacities. By studying these components of the environment, their values in terms of degrees of rarity, and their capacity to resist and regenerate from natural and man-made effects, it has been possible to produce maps of environmental thresholds and capacities for various activities. For example, capacities for hiking, skiing or fishing have been produced in much the same way as other forms of threshold analysis. Territorial ultimate environmental thresholds have been mapped to indicate areas from which certain activities should be excluded. Within the remainder of the study area, quantitative ultimate environmental thresholds indicate levels of development that should not be exceeded by particular forms of tourist activity expressed in the maximum number of users. Temporal thresholds include activities at certain times, for example during breeding season or when there is a high water table and soil instability.

Threshold analysis has therefore been developed into a versatile technique for identifying desirable levels of activities where these activities involve using several resources. Each resource is considered in terms of its capacity and possibilities for expansion or substitution and from this, overall optimum levels of activity can be identified. It is quite possible that the same principles could be extended to other fields perhaps in manpower planning or in transport planning for example.

8 Plan making for an inner city district: Small Heath, Birmingham

Plan and policy making is usually both remedial and opportunistic. Solutions are sought for problems and opportunities to realise site potentials are sought also. Often, the realisation of an opportunity is also a partial solution to a local problem - for example, an industrial development which provides jobs locally. Sometimes it is not closely related to a local problem - for example an industrial development employing labour from outside. Invariably it is a question of emphasis, whether the prime consideration is to address a local problem or to emphasise the exploitation of local potential (which may itself provide revenue or other side effects to address other local issues).

Where there are many constraints and local problems, as in an inner city district such as Small Heath in Birmingham, problems will generally receive more emphasis than opportunities. Certainly the pursuit of goals and objectives may prove to be an approach of less immediate relevance than addressing problems, though much depends on how the goals and objectives are constituted.

Throughout this chapter the references to Small Heath are only selective, not exhaustive. Issues, objectives, policy alternatives and in fact all the illustrative references to Small Heath represent only a fraction of the possibilities, selected to illustrate approaches and methods of preparing

Figure 8.1   The railway line separates Small Heath to the north-east (right) from Sparkbrook to the south-west (left).   The City Centre is about 2½km distant.

Figure 8.2   To the east, playing fields bordering the River Cole separate Small Heath (left) from Hay Mills.

policies and plans, rather than to prepare a document for Small Heath, such as the Small Heath District Plan (Birmingham City Council 1976 and 1981).

ISSUES AND OPPORTUNITIES IN SMALL HEATH

For many districts it is a common interest of problems, issues and opportunities which help to define the boundary of the area. These may be considered together with physical boundaries such as railway lines, canals and changes in land uses. Roads such as high-speed dual carriageways may be boundaries; roads with a continuous shopping or commercial frontage may be centres for the local area. Local government or other administrative areas are frequently defined on narrow, single-purpose criteria and may define planning areas only by coincidence. Small Heath Ward does not coincide.

In Small Heath, the railway line with extensive sidings forms a clear physical boundary to the south-west. To the south-east the former Birmingham Small Arms factory site separates communities looking towards the shopping frontage along Coventry Road in Small Heath from those closer to a distinct but comparable area further east on Coventry Road in Yardley. To the north-east the boundary is less clear. Small Heath merges into communities looking towards Bordesley Green with many common issues and problems. Changes in land uses towards extensive, large scale industries and the main Birmingham-London railway line may be considered as boundary criteria, though they are at some distance from the main uniting element in Small Heath - the district centre uses along Coventry Road. To the north-west the primary residential and small scale industry and commerce of Small Heath gives way to the predominantly industrial district of Bordesley.

Issues, problems and opportunities may be thought of as either being primarily confined to Small Heath or as involving Small Heath in a role extending to neighbouring districts, the south-eastern sector of the City or wider.

Issues linking Small Heath and a wider area

These may be divided into issues where Small Heath may have a role to play in relation to policies for the City as a whole, for example by providing industrial sites to promote city-wide employment opportunities and where Small Heath's role is due to its location, for example in acting as a traffic corridor.

Figure 8.3 To the west, Small Heath borders on the industrial
district of Bordesley with the City Centre 1km away.

Figure 8.4 Much of the remaining industry in Small Heath is in
the south-east; Council estate to the north-east.

Figures 8.5 & 8.6 In recent years, some important industries
have been lost such as the Talbot Car Factory
(above) and the BSA works (foreground below).

Figure 8.7 Some new industry has been attracted, especially in the south-east, helped by investments in infra-structure such as Small Heath By-Pass (foreground).

Figure 8.8 Some important industries have been retained.

<u>Industrial sites for the City as a whole</u> Some of the
questions to be addressed are as follows:

- To whom might this be an issue? City Council, County
  Council, Central Government, local residents, ratepayers,
  industrialists (local and regional)? job seekers?

- Why might it be an issue? Increase in employment
  opportunities; opportunities for industrialists; increase
  in rateable value; increase in taxes paid.

- Why might it be worth attention? Are sites available
  elsewhere? Opportunities for environmental improvement
  with industrial development? Need to protect the
  environment particularly from heavy goods vehicles and
  pollution.

- What powers are available to promote industry and who would
  use them? Grants and subsidies; co-ordination of
  infrastructure; compulsory purchase of land and assembly of
  suitable sites; advertisement of opportunities; agreements
  under section 52 of the Town and Country Planning Act 1971.

Discussion of possible action by the City Council on the
economic and employment situation in Small Heath is contained
in Smith (1976).

<u>Issues within Small Heath</u> No issues are strictly confined
within Small Heath in the sense that the well-being of any
district will always have some effect on the city as a whole.
Also, nearly all the issues in an area such as Small Heath are
repeated in neighbouring districts and many of them in other
cities. However, there are issues which can be addressed from
the point of view of local rather than wider needs. For
example:

<u>Decline of Coventry Road shopping</u> The main shopping area of
Small Heath stretches along both sides of Coventry Road and
acts as a meeting place for the district.

- To whom might this be an issue? All local shoppers but
  particularly those less mobile, some local job seekers,
  local traders, local authority.

- Why might it be an issue and why might it be worth
  attention? Inconvenience, hardship for some, loss of
  competition and business to traders (when shopping
  generally declines there is usually more business lost by
  fewer customers visiting the area than business gained to

101

Figure 8.9   Old, obsolescent or underused buildings and land
in temporary and not very intensive use are
characteristic of much of Small Heath.

Figure 8.10   Coventry Road is the main focal point of Small
Heath as well as a main radial route from the
City and has a variety of commercial premises.

102

Figures 8.11 & 8.12 Basically late Victorian, there has been
a lot of post-War redevelopment and infilling
especially at the western end of Coventry Road.

Figures 8.13 & 8.14   The children at Small Heath schools come
from various cultural traditions and there have
been problems of achieving fluency in English.

those remaining due to loss of competition), social effects of the decline of a meeting place; loss of rates revenue to local authority (there may be some gain too by shops moving elsewhere); loss of jobs; loss of business and perhaps jobs to firms servicing the shops, for example window cleaners, accountants, stationers.

- What powers are available to prevent the decline and who would use them? Adjustment of rates payable to local authority; environmental improvements financed by local and central government; prevention of shopping competition elsewhere by local planning authority; control of through traffic by highway authority; provision of car parking and public transport for shoppers by local authority and West Midlands Passenger Transport Executive (public transport is already good); provision of other attractive facilities nearby such as Small Heath Community School.

Low levels of educational achievement (see Morton-Williams and Stowell 1974)

- To whom might this be an issue? Schoolchildren, parents, employees, local education authority. Due to the effects of educational achievement on job and other opportunities, it will also be of concern to a much wider spectrum of organisations not directly concerned with education, for example the police, social services department, careers service, churches.

- Why might it be an issue? Restriction of job opportunities and self-fulfilment; unsuitable labour force; unwillingness of many English speaking families to send their children to schools where a substantial proportion of the children do not speak English and consequent unwillingness to live in Small Heath; low educational aspirations and their inter-relationships with low aspirations and achievement in employment, unemployment and other societal relationships; higher costs of education due to fewer pupils per teacher than average in Birmingham, needed because of language and other problems; home liaison, community development staff; special allowances for teachers in designated schools; careers service; absenteeism from school; movement out of Small Heath of most of the few able pupils.

- Why might it be worth attention? Improvement and self-fulfilment of local schoolchildren; reduction of likelihood of side-effects such as vandalism, violence and other crime and anti-social behaviour; increased contribution to local and wider society and economy.

Figure 8.15 Several of the schools in Small Heath were built
in the late Victorian or Edwardian periods and
are of considerable architectural interest.

Figure 8.16 An older junior and infant school remains
opposite Small Heath School and Community Centre.

- What powers are available to raise educational achievement and who might use them? An increase in investment from central and local government might have some effect; so too might an increase in staff. An increase in job opportunities might increase motivation of pupils. Acceptance of English as a common language by Asian and other non-British families (the Community Federation expressed concern about the high proportion of non-English speaking children in Small Heath during the preparation of the District Plan (Birmingham City Council 1976)).

The statistical methods explained in chapters 4 and 5 will be useful for analysing issues to determine the strengths of relationships between suspected causes and effects. In addition, cluster analysis may also help to show which factors group most closely together to explain an observed phenomenon. In order to use this technique, it is first necessary to calculate correlation coefficients between pairs of variables. For example, the number of dwellings lacking at least one standard amenity and the number in the private rented sector can be obtained for each enumeration district from the 1981 Census. Pearson's product moment correlation coefficient may be calculated as follows:

$$\text{correlation coefficient} = \frac{\dfrac{\sum x_i y_i - \bar{x}\bar{y}}{n}}{\sigma_x \cdot \sigma_y}$$

where x_i, y_i refer to numbers of dwellings lacking at least one standard amenity and in the private rented sector

     $\bar{x}$, $\bar{y}$ are the means of these for all enumeration districts included

     n is the number of enumeration districts

     σ_x σ_y are the standard deviations of x and y

Cluster analysis is a method of identifying which variables from a whole series are most strongly related from which it is usually assumed that they share something in common. It is frequently used in relation to housing conditions and social services. For example the following correlation coefficients were obtained in a survey of an inner city area.

Figure 8.17   Much of Birmingham's pre-1914 housing has now
been improved under the Envelope Scheme (see
also Figure 5.8.

Figure 8.18   Small Heath School and Community Centre,
completed early 1978 and including a six-form
entry secondary school, swimming pool, sports
hall, library, drama studio, youth club and bar.

houses		1	2	3	4	5	6	7
lacking 1+ amenities	1		0.60	0.71	0.24	0.52	0.23	0.42
in need of repair	2	0.60		0.24	0.14	0.57	0.22	0.39
RV < £175	3	0.71	0.24		0.27	0.31	0.16	0.44
no car	4	0.24	0.14	0.27		0.14	0.17	0.26
privately rented	5	0.52	0.57	0.31	0.14		0.20	0.31
social services cases	6	0.23	0.22	0.16	0.17	0.20		0.45
shared dwelling	7	0.42	0.39	0.44	0.26	0.31	0.45	

In each column the highest correlation is marked. The highest pair is identified (0.71 between 1 and 3). Both of these must have a higher correlation with each other than with any others. They are a reciprocal pair and form the core of a cluster, which is noted as $1 \rightleftarrows 3 \atop (0.71)$

The rows for each reciprocal pair are checked to see if any of the correlations are marked as the highest in their columns. We see that for row 1, column 2 is the highest and for row 3, column 4 is the highest.

$$2 \underset{(0.60)}{\longrightarrow} 1 \underset{(0.71)}{\rightleftarrows} 3 \underset{(0.27)}{\longrightarrow} 4$$

Variables involved in such a correlation have a higher correlation with one of the variables of the reciprocal pair than with any other variable.

The rows of the new members of the cluster (2 and 4) are then checked to see if any of the correlations are marked as highest in their columns. For row 2 we see column 5 is highest, but there are none for row 4. The cluster now becomes as follows

$$5 \underset{(0.57)}{\longrightarrow} 2 \underset{(0.60)}{\longrightarrow} 1 \underset{(0.71)}{\rightleftarrows} 3 \underset{(0.27)}{\longrightarrow} 4$$

Row 5 is then checked and we see that no variable is marked as highest in its column. The cluster is therefore complete.

The remaining variables are then searched for further reciprocal pairs, i.e. two variables which have a higher correlation with each other than with any other variables. In the above case we see 6 and 7 are reciprocal.

Figures 8.19 & 8.20 The School and Community Centre was one
of the initiatives of the late 1970s intended to
put Small Heath on its feet. Housing treatment
under the Envelope Scheme continued some of the
same aims into the 1980s.

$$6 \underset{(0.45)}{\overset{\longrightarrow}{\rightleftharpoons}} 7$$

Checking the rows for 6 and 7 we see no others show the highest correlation in their columns and so this second cluster extends no further.

GOALS AND OBJECTIVES

In a district such as Small Heath where most planning is orientated towards problems, goals and objectives may have two main uses:

- to help clarify priorities between issues and the measures which address them. Each goal or objective will relate to only one or a limited range of issues and therefore to get a true picture of priorities, a complete list of goals and objectives would have to be studied. Examples that will help decision making in some circumstances are as follows:

  'To encourage private sector investment which will provide employment or other community benefits'.

  'To provide closer contact and understanding between the schools and families and the neighbourhoods which they serve' (see Llewelyn-Davies et al 1977).

  'To improve personal services and encourage and enable people to help themselves' (see Birmingham City Council 1980).

  'To reduce the amount of obsolescent land and buildings'.

- to act as guiding principles in case of dispute such as in development control. Policies will generally be used for this purpose but there may also be circumstances when reference will be made to the goals and objectives which influenced the policies. Examples for a district such as Small Heath might include the following:

  'To provide choice of tenure for low income groups' (see Llewelyn-Davies et al 1976).

  'To maintain Coventry Road as the main focal point of the District; to maintain Coventry Road as a major shopping area; to allow conversion of shopping to non-shopping uses only in exceptional circumstances'.

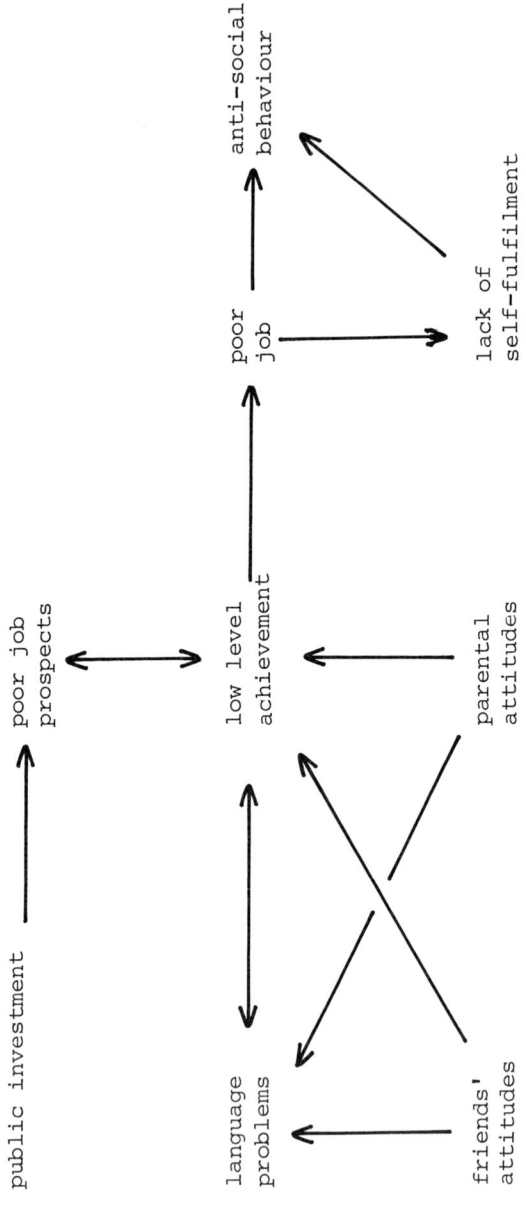

Figure 8.21 Possible inter-relationships between some issues in Small Heath

Goals, objectives and policies often merge into each other without clear distinction between them.

Goals may also provide guidance in preparing alternative policies and plans at a later stage. For example cash-and-carry warehousing away from Coventry Road may be a way of achieving development compatible with a goal of encouraging private sector investment which will provide employment. At the same time it would go against an objective of maintaining Coventry Road as a shopping area. A series of goals and objectives usually imply policy choices and it is these choices which are expressed as alternatives.

DATA ANALYSIS

A first step to identify data requirements may be made by tracing out the implications and interrelationships of the issues. Figure 8.21 is an example of how this may be started. Each topic or issue shown will be translated into quantitative and/or qualitative indicators. For example, poor job prospects may be represented by the number of jobs, wages offered, a qualitative assessment of likely job satisfaction and the likely number of applicants. Similarly, language problems may be represented by achievement of school children in reading, writing and conversation tests.

The arrows represent only the relationships which are expected. Whether these do in fact occur will be tested by applying to the data assembled for the issues and topics statistical techniques such as Pearson's product moment correlation coefficient, the Phi distribution or the Point Biserial correlation coefficient depending on the form of data available. Although as was discussed in chapter 2, there are clear and important distinctions between correlation and cause, a network approach to correlation analysis, particularly if supported by multi-variate analysis can reduce the risk of mistaking causes.

Correlation techniques help to establish whether a relationship exists between variables. To quantify this relationship and predict the effects of a change in an independent variable on a dependent variable, regression analysis should be used.

For example, using the indices already explained for language problems and poor job prospects: suppose it was found that the mean for the language index was 3.5 units and for job prospects 4.9 with standard deviations of 1.02 and 4.45

Figures 8.22 & 8.23   A new junior, infant and nursery school
in the western part of Small Heath.

respectively, and that the correlation coefficient had been previously calculated to be 0.74. The equation of the straight line of regression can be calculated as

$$y - 4.9 = 0.74 \quad .(4.45/1.02)(x-3.5)$$

where language is the x variable and job prospects the y variable.

$$y = 3.23x - 6.40$$

In this way it is possible to start to assess the effects of change in one variable on the other, for example the effects of investment in language teaching on job prospects. In reality of course, the situation will be far more complex. Each factor is not only influenced by one other - it is influenced by several. Also the relationship may not be a straight line one. For solutions to these and other related problems the reader is referred to more advanced statistics texts such as Yeomans (1968), Hope (1968), Lawley and Maxwell (1971), Press (1972), Blalock (1972), Comrey (1973), Morrisson (1976), Wright (1979), Spiegel (1980) and Draper and Smith (1981).

Understanding the causes and interrelationships between issues is an essential step in plan or policy making. Without this, investment or other remedial treatment may be no more effective than throwing effort and money on a bonfire. The causes of the existing problem may consume the new initiatives just as they gave rise to the problem in the first place. Effort and money should always be aimed at causes rather than effects or symptoms. Regression analysis can be a very useful starting point for predicting the effects of change of one factor, perhaps a policy change, on others in the network. It can help to identify where within the network investment would be most effective in achieving policy aims, a fundamental and indispensable part of policy formulation. This is why techniques to help describe and explain causes and to quantify relationships are so important.

The methods of data analysis mentioned so far are to explain the extent of the issues, what might be called the demand side for planned action. On the other hand there will be a need for assessment of the state of the study area and what might be needed to meet these demands - how the study area may be used to supply some partial answers. Many of the traditional planning surveys will come within this category. These include land use and condition surveys and surveys of the quantity and quality of the various facilities such as

Figures 8.24 & 8.25 The environment of Small Heath is very
                     poor in some parts, with considerable areas of
                     vacant land and scrap yards.

schools, shops or jobs which will be identified in analysis of the issues.

Most of the techniques used in survey will be traditional, descriptive maps or tables. AIDA (chapter 7) may prove useful for setting out the considerations and feasible alternatives for a site or group of sites or the future of a redundant school or other facility giving rise to action in some form. Care, however, will be needed not to apply it too mechanically and waste a lot of time and perhaps computer facilities by analysing a lot of alternatives which are 'non-starters' for reasons which would be revealed by a thorough knowledge of the area.

FORECASTING AND IDENTIFICATION OF AREAS OF UNCERTAINTY

Forecasting can be an attempt to predict what will happen or as an effort to exert influence on those able to bring about a desired action such as the granting of subsidies. Certainly the first of these activities will not be as prominent in problem-orientated planning as in Small Heath as in planning for the realisation of opportunities. This is because what already exists is sufficient to justify extensive immediate action. Future changes may intensify this need or reduce it, but either way it would become apparent as implementation takes place. Such a situation is quite different from one where large scale new development is envisaged which will be dependent on forecasted needs. In Small Heath, the needs are those of the present, as well as those of the future.

There may however, be exceptions. Forecasting of the needs for some facilities which are very strongly and closely related to the number of people, for example schools, will still be important. Forecasting future rates of house building or renovation or rates of job creation will take second place to efforts to provide them. Estimation of the viability of any new shopping will certainly be an important task both for developer and local authority as will be the effects of any new competitive shopping such as cash-and-carry warehouses nearby.

Identifying areas of uncertainty is for the purpose of showing which policies or proposals need to be most flexible and adaptable to unforseen changes, and perhaps also which need further survey. In an area such as Small Heath, uncertainty relating to the total extent of development or treatment desirable will not be as important as the need for immediate action to make a start. As for most aspects of

Figure 8.26   Much of the vacant or little-used land is behind
the frontages of the main roads.

Figure 8.27   The Mixed Urban Farm is a worthwhile attempt to
make this part of Small Heath more attractive.

forecasting, the present is enough to justify action and also the future is to a large extent dependent on what is planned and the reactions of local residents.

PREPARATION OF ALTERNATIVE PLANS AND POLICIES

Alternatives will be determined from:

- what is feasible site by site; physical size, effects on neighbours, access, presence of infrastructure, appearance, commercial viability of the location (for some developments)
- what seems to be most effective in solving the kind of problem described in Figure 8.21. It is uncertainty as to what might be most effective which will result in alternative policies or proposals. Presentation of alternatives may illustrate the uncertainty and promote further discussion by politicians, public and professional officers
- goals and objectives which may give some guidance on priorities.

Alternatives will be of two fairly distinct kinds - alternative proposals site by site and alternative policies or ways of reacting to issues and promoting their solution.

It is still common practice to draw large zones as being 'primarily industrial' or 'primarily residential with ancillary uses'. Any vacant or derelict land is then allocated to the appropriate category. Although certainly the immediately adjacent uses will influence zoning, mixing of land uses can lead to advantages of easier access to jobs and perhaps even the environmental variety may be appreciated in some circumstances.

The criteria for preparing alternatives for a given site will depend on how much uncertainty there is. Where there is a lot of uncertainty, the alternatives may be completely different uses, perhaps industry, housing and open space. Frequently, however, public and politician contributions to the understanding of issues and objectives and site surveys will remove enough of this uncertainty for the alternatives to be within one major land use category - alternative forms and density of housing for example. Even the breadth of variation within a criterion such as density may be limited by reference to issues and their expression in policies and what is feasible on the site by reference to size, access, and desired spacing between buildings for example.

Figures 8.28 & 8.29   The arrival of building society premises
in Birmingham inner residential districts is
really a trend of the 1980s.

Figures 8.30 & 8.31 Simultaneously with the arrival of
building societies there has been an awakening
of interest by private sector housing developers.

Figure 8.32   For many years up to the early 1980s most of the
new-build housing was by the Council or by
housing associations and the latter continues.

Figure 8.33   Small Heath Park is a welcome green space in this
densely built-up area.

Like plans, alternative policies may refer to radically different or to only quite marginally different choices. The Consultants to the Inner Area Study, Llewelyn-Davies, Weeks, Forestier-Walker and Bor, expressed in the project report the alternatives of either rehabilitation and improvement for present income groups or an active policy of encouraging higher income groups to move in (Llewelyn-Davies et al 1974). This may have seemed an unlikely prospect over most of Small Heath but in the 1980s a considerable amount of private sector housing has been built and sold for what by Small Heath standards, is a higher than average local price.

Other alternatives will be much more specific in their application than this. For example, low educational achievement could be addressed by an combination of measures applied to the factors shown to influence it which might include those represented in Figure 8.21. Some guidance on the likely effectiveness of the very large number of alternatives possible may be forthcoming from studies to analyse the strengths of these relationships.

CONCLUSIONS

Understanding of the relationships between issues is the key to identifying where planned action will address causes of problems rather than be frittered away patching up the effects. Statistical and other planning methods will help to test whether the hunches and speculations (hypotheses) of politicians, planners and pressure groups have much validity. Planning methods might even help to spark off some of these ideas for testing but they will never do so without local knowledge.

An alternative approach to the one taken here, which is issue-centred, would be to centre attention on groups of people within Small Heath - Asian teenagers, the elderly, schoolchildren, young parents, for example. The issues and problems of Small Heath seen from the perspective of each group may be a more direct and effective approach to some kinds of planning than the one suggested in this chapter. A problem of this kind of approach is how to fit the whole population into valid categories which share common views of the District. There is a danger of some being neglected or even being discriminated against by this approach. Another problem is that most planned action is not aimed at only one group.

Either approach will rely for its effectiveness on a co-ordinated effort covering a wide range of policies other than those of the statutory planning system centred on the Town and Country Planning Acts. This may have the co-ordinating role in that such planning documents take heed of the views, work and powers of the whole range of other officials. However, town and country planning alone can only be effective when there is either a lot of public investment to be planned or where there is a lot of demand for development by the private sector when development control becomes effective. In a situation like present-day Small Heath where there is neither, there is the need to use rating and tax policies, and the resources of a whole spectrum of social service, education, housing and other interests if the policies are to be implemented effectively.

9 Evaluation of alternative plans and policies

For two decades or more there have been two apparently distinct, sometimes seen as almost rival approaches to evaluation in planning - Lichfield's Planning Balance Sheet (Lichfield, Kettle and Whitbread 1975) and Hill's Goals Achievement Matrix (Hill 1968). Both have been fairly frequently used and the Goals Achievement Matrix has been a common approach in Structure Plan Evaluation (Booth and Jaffe 1978).

Basically the Planning Balance Sheet is a cost-benefit approach with costs and benefits disaggregated according to who gains and who pays. The Goals Achievement Matrix was a response to what Hill saw as a deficiency of the Planning Balance Sheet - an alleged lack of attention to the purposes behind achieving the benefits or the achievement of goals. After the appearance of the Goals Achievement Matrix it is true that the Planning Balance Sheet changed quite significantly in form to accommodate these and other criticisms. However, the differences between the two approaches are perhaps not as great as are sometimes portrayed. Progress towards goals or objectives could be accounted for in a cost-benefit approach in the measurement of the costs and benefits. These would be part of considering consumer surplus and interpersonal comparisons of utility.

An approach to evaluation based on the measurement of the

achievement of goals is only as credible as our ability to specify goals and to measure progression towards them in a medium which is comparable from one goal to another. Techniques which do not use money as the medium of measurement seem to be prone to a great deal of theoretical and practical scepticism (Simpson 1975). The problems of specifying goals and the inadequacies of a goal-orientated approach in many planning situations including those in Small Heath, may be no more than a semantic obstacle. Without radical alteration a Goals Achievement Matrix could become a Problem Solution Matrix.

No matter what approach is used there will be a series of questions and problems which are always liable to be relevant in choosing between alternatives, whether they are alternative proposals for a site or building, alternative ways of going about a task or alternative policies. These are the problems of cost and benefit measurement, costs and benefits being defined in a very wide sense. Certainly benefit measurement should include consideration of progression towards goals and solution of problems. Cost measurement could involve consideration of how resources used for one alternative may prevent the progression to goals or solution of problems that would occur if investment was made in another alternative.

There are many useful references on cost and benefit measurement and analysis. Some of those which explain principles are Pearce (1971), Mishan (1975) and Dasgupta and Pearce (1978). Others which analyse principles more closely to a planning context are Schreiber, Gatons and Clemmer (1971), Kendall (1971), Georgi (1973), Bovaird (1978) and Morriss (1983).

RULES FOR CHOOSING BETWEEN PROJECTS

There are several ways of looking at costs and benefits, each resulting in a different rule for decision making:

A) As a result of carrying out project A, project B must be abandoned. The costs of project A are therefore the same magnitude as the benefits of project B. The decision making rule is 'carry out project A if its benefits exceed the benefits forgone by not carrying out project B'.

B) Costs and benefits should be summed for the whole of the life of a project. The rule then is to select all projects for which the present value of the benefits exceeds the present value of the costs.

C) The rate of return of a project (p) is the rate which results in the present value of a project being 0.

$$0 = B_o - C_o + \frac{B_i - C_i}{1 + p} \cdots\cdots\cdots \frac{B_n + C_n}{(1 + p)^n}$$

The discount rate of a project is the rate which reflects the preference for consumption of goods at the present over consumption of exactly similar goods in the future.

The rule for decision making is 'undertake the project if the rate of return exceeds the discount rate'.

ESTIMATING COSTS AND BENEFITS AT THE TIME THAT THEY OCCUR

In comparing planning projects, it is invariably the case that many costs and benefits are not measurable in any medium - the 'intangibles'. Let us consider, for example, two hypothetical alternative policies for shopping along Coventry Road in Small Heath:

A) To refuse planning permission for conversion of shops to other uses.
B) To refuse planning permission for conversion of shops to other uses except building society offices.

In drawing up a list of costs and benefits for each policy several might fall within the realm of the intangibles, for example:

B) benefits - convenience to local residents, encouragement of building societies to grant mortgages locally, creation of jobs prospects, visual improvement.

Also there will be costs and benefits which are measurable only in various incomparable media. For example, time in hours and minutes is a very frequent item in planning projects resulting from a change in land use causing different patterns of movement. Although (with difficulty) it may be measurable, the problem is to compare it with those costs and benefits involving monetary exchanges such as the costs of construction. There is quite a large and useful literature on the valuation of time, for example Harrison and Quarmby (1969), Layard (1973), Mansfield (1971), Roth (1967). Various methods have been devised for measuring the extent to which time has been substituted for money and money for time by

observing and asking about travel behaviour. Choice of route
to avoid tolls or choice of mode of travel where there are
both time and fare differences have been considered. Trade
offs between time and money have been observed in these ways.

Another common example in planning of a cost which is
measurable but difficult to evaluate is that of noise. This
is often associated with projects involving building such as
for industry or warehousing or perhaps even more important,
road construction.

Inadequacies of market values

A) <u>Consumers' surplus</u> People are often willing to pay more
for an item than they are required to. If the price of
installing an electricity supply rose sharply, most
householders or industrialists would be willing to pay more
rather than be without. The difference between the maximum
that a person is willing to pay and what is actually paid is
the consumers' surplus. One may wonder whether investment
should take place in items or projects where consumers'
surplus is high rather than where it is low. This might give
the best returns in the form of high consumer satisfaction.
Whilst this is true for some projects, it is certainly not
always the case. Most infrastructure projects, including
electricity supply can be expected to give high consumer
surplus, but once each building is connected, consumer surplus
from further investment would be small or nil. For some
projects, such as road construction and improvement on the
other other hand, there will be no such 'threshold' of
consumer satisfaction. There is more scope for improved
connections giving some marginal satisfaction.

The underlying problem for project evaluation is that market
prices do not represent true values. Even the costs and
benefits apparently measurable, such as those of construction
are measurable only in a partial and arbitrary way.

The principles of consumers' surplus are applicable also in
situations other than investment in goods. Returning to our
example of the two hypothetical alternative shopping policies
for Coventry Road in Small Heath, one benefit of allowing
building societies might be creation of improved job
prospects. Just as a person might enjoy some consumer surplus
in buying goods, an employee might enjoy some surplus in
salary - a surplus above the minimum he or she would accept
for the job. It is to be expected that whatever this surplus
might be, it is likely to vary according to the kind of job.

Often in evaluation it is important to decide whether to measure the costs resulting from an action or development or the benefits. For example, accessibility is usually measured in terms of the costs of fares, fuel, time, inconvenience and discomfort of travel. Presumably these are at least matched by the benefits gained on arrival at the destination. Perhaps there will be some consumer surplus. SETRA (1974) have argued that measurement of costs alone is unsufficient. When an improved transport route is introduced there is usually a tendency to travel further than to travel the same distance and save time. Given the choice, travellers often prefer to open up a wider range of destinations and their opportunities and benefits rather than to save time. A second example supports the same conclusion. Small neighbouring towns have been observed to develop not independently but with increasing interconnections. Alternatively one may develop to a greater extent than the others. The development form which would minimise travel time - independent development - seems to take place quite rarely. These examples both point to the conclusion that where possible, measurement of benefits may be more valid than measurement of costs because benefits will include an element of consumers' surplus. The same reasoning is reflected in the gravity model where interactions are explained in terms of attractiveness of destination as well as general costs of transport.

B) <u>Average production cost or marginal production cost?</u> The market price of many goods reflect the cost of production rather than the benefits to consumers. For some goods such as housing, production costs generally represent a base-line, though certainly where there are high profits, these are partly the result of the realisation of consumer surplus. The situation is, however, usually far more complex. Competition from housing being available elsewhere will prevent the developer (and landowner) reaping the full consumer surplus. Agreements under section 52 of the Town and Country Planning Act 1971 may result in some housing being sold at below cost, in order to obtain a profitable planning permission elsewhere.

However, if we may set these complications aside for a moment, there still arises the question of whether projects should reflect the costs of providing the actual goods involved (marginal production cost) or a share of the total costs of production (average production cost). Railway fares and in fact most services tend to reflect the latter. The cost of carrying an extra passenger on a scheduled train (marginal cost) would be extremely small.

The significance of this question for planning projects is

that if average production cost is charged and this greatly exceeds marginal production cost (a very common situation for services) then the goods may never be produced. The value to the consumer may lie between the two. This may be significant because if extra customers (consumers) are prevented from taking part, economies of scale may be forgone, as well as the revenue not received from the potential consumers. The possibility of reducing average production cost and therefore cost to existing customers is lost. This could have been prevented by charging more than marginal production cost but no more than this plus consumers' surplus.

These principles will perhaps apply most closely and most significantly in planning projects which involve charging for services, such as the pricing of sports facilities.

C) <u>Unemployment, taxes and employment subsidies</u> A large part of the costs of many projects is made up of wages and employment taxes such as income tax and National Insurance contributions. Much of that which reaches employees is spent on goods subject to VAT and services which again involve income taxes and National Insurance contributions. The published cost of a public sector project is usually a grossly distorted overestimate of its true monetary cost. For private sector projects it may be closer to the true cost from one viewpoint, that of the promoter or developer. In a similar way as taxes overestimate the cost of a project, employment subsidies may lead to the costs being underestimated.

The true cost of a project should reflect the benefits that would result from the projects which would have used the same labour and which have to be foregone. Quite frequently there are no alternative projects. The project relieves unemployment and the true costs are small.

The problems for project evaluation arise when these factors apply differently between the alternatives. Returning to the two hypothetical shopping policies for Coventry Road Small Heath, it is possible that they would have different employment implications in terms of numbers of jobs, taxes and National Insurance contributions and in the relief of unemployment. This might be not only directly in terms of the employees of the shops and building societies but also indirectly in terms of any other employment which might follow. Both shops and building societies might need the services of window cleaners or accountants for example. Building societies might help stimulate house building within the district. Also, building societies receive a large amount of state protection in terms of income tax relief to their borrowers which will have a similar effect to an employment subsidy.

D) <u>Monopolies</u> Monopolies may have an important effect on prices in planning projects. The availability of labour certainly influences wages. Similarly, many goods such as utility services, including water, gas and electricity for practical purposes are monopolistic. Even where there are alternatives, as for heating, taxes on cheaper methods, in this case gas, makes market prices artificially high so that an alternative such as electricity will remain competitive. Monopolies may permit excess profits, hide inefficiences, yield high taxes or provide for investment which would not otherwise be possible.

Monopolies often exist for state-provided services (though since 1979 there have been efforts to reduce these, or threats of 'privatisation' depending on your political viewpoint). The effects of monopolies in planning evaluation may be expected to be most significant in comparison of policies involving services provided by local or central government. Site servicing although mostly monopolistic generally does not result in high costs. In fact service connection charges are usually below marginal cost, as connection charges are usually subsidised from sales afterwards.

E) <u>The problem of the second best</u> Much theoretical discussion has taken place on what criterion should be used for an increase in economic welfare which would make a project worthwhile. See for example Kaldor (1939), Hicks (1939), Little (1958), Phelps (Ed) (1973), Layard (Ed) (1973). One of the most widely accepted criterion is to the effect that a project should go ahead if the gainers could compensate the losers even if they do not actually do so. In practice, attempts usually are made to compensate losers by measures such as taxes and planning gain where social goods such as open space may be a condition of getting planning permission. Much of the compensation is very indirect. It is paid in social goods such as Small Heath Community Centre financed out of taxes.

The problem in project evaluation is that goods produced under conditions which do not maximise economic welfare make market measures of costs and benefits distorted valuations of economic welfare. The prices of building materials, plant hire and labour for example all influence the cost of a project. If any of these inputs are not produced under conditions which maximise economic welfare, then the price or cost which is charged to the project will result in the transference of that distortion to the evaluation of the project itself, unless adjustments are made to the costs taken into account.

It is hard to imagine a planning project or policy which does not involve labour. They usually involve choice between one kind of job and another such as between building society cashiers and shop assistants when there will be gainers and losers resulting from policies. This opens up many of the problems of the second best in policy evaluation.

<u>Frozen Costs</u> Some investments necessarily lie unused whilst a project is being undertaken. Whilst housing is being built for example, mains services such as water, drainage, gas, electricity and roads will remain under-used or unused until the houses are occupied. Certain sections of a road may lie idle until other parts have been completed. When a large development is in progress and building rates are slow and when interest rates are high, these investments lying idle and the interest payable on them may make the difference between a project being viable and not so, or they could be decisive in choosing between alternative projects.

Example - Initial investment for servicing an estate of 400 houses is £300,000. If the completion rate is 100 houses per year and the interest payable on the services 10% per year, frozen costs may be calculated as follows:

			£
Year 1	investment lying idle	£300,000 @ 10%	30,000
Year 2		$\dfrac{£300,000 \times 3 @ 10\%}{4}$	22,500
Year 3		$\dfrac{£300,000 \times 2 @ 10\%}{4}$	15,000
Year 4		$\dfrac{£300,000 @ 10\%}{4}$	7,500
		Total frozen cost	£75,000

In choosing between large and small developments and in the phasing of large developments the choice is between high frozen costs and foregoing economies of scale.

DISCOUNT RATES

Costs an benefits occur throughout the life of a project.   The problem is what allowance is to be made for goods received now in preference to an equal amount of goods received in the future. It is usually acknowledged that goods and services are preferred sooner rather than later. Returns received sooner can be put to work or to earn interest. Consumer behaviour however, reveals more complicated motives. Banks and building societies still receive deposits when their interest rates are below the level of inflation. This however, does not solve the problem. In fact it makes it more complicated and difficult to derive a discount rate (which would be negative if preference really was for future over present consumption).

Example

		Project A £	Project B £
Year 1	costs	1000	600
2	costs	110	550
3	benefits	100	50
4	benefits	100	100
5	benefits	100	150

Adding the costs and benefits for the first five years gives us net costs of £810 for project A and £850 for project B. If we assumed an interest rate of 10% on costs however, the value in year 1 of project A costs for year 2 would be reduced to £100. Similarly year 2 costs for project B would also be reduced so that their year 1 value becomes £500. (In both cases, the value in year 1 is that value which would become the year 2 value by the addition of 10% i.e. year 2 value multiplied by 10/11). Taking into account the preference for paying costs later rather than sooner therefore reduces the net costs of the projects to £800 each.

If benefits are preferred by 5% simple rate per year, to account those for the two projects in terms of year 1 values we must reduce them as follows:

		project A £	project B £
Year 3	benefits	100 - 10 = 90	50 - 5 = 45
Year 4	benefits	100 - 15 = 85	100 - 15 = 85
Year 5	benefits	100 - 20 = 80	150 - 22.5 = 127.5

Year 3 benefits are to be reduced by 2 years at 5% simple rate = 10%.
The project A benefits are therefore reduced to £255 and project B to £257.5.

The net costs of project A and project B, reduced to year 1 values would therefore become £845 and £842.5 respectively. This method of cost discounting may be regarded as a way of estimating the net costs if all the investment was available at the beginning of the project, but some was not used immediately and was invested to earn interest. This interest earned is to be deducted from the cost disbursed. The costs and benefits are all estimated to a common time, the start of the project, for sake of comparison in accordance with rules B and C for choosing betweeen projects (see pages 126-7).

In project or policy appraisal or in evaluating alternatives, discount rates for costs may be estimated by reference to rates of interests for investments. For many projects there will be uncertainty about future rates that will have to be paid. In estimating discount rates for benefits on the other hand, there are no market rates to which reference can be made. As already mentioned, consumer behaviour is rather contradictory in this respect. Certainly there are situations where it reveals a negative discount rate - future consumption is preferred to the present. There may also be planning situations where it is more realistic to regard immediate action (and therefore benefits) as essential rather than preferable, for example care for the elderly.

INTERPERSONAL COMPARISONS OF UTILITY

If the costs and benefits for two projects A and B could be estimated accurately and found to be the same it does not necessarily follow that there are no grounds for choice between them. Different groups of people may be affected. It is generally acknowledged that benefits to a wealthy person are less valuable than equal benefits to someone less wealthy. The marginal values of costs and benefits will be different for every person affected by a planning project or policy. The problem is how to quantify these differences or at least acknowledge their existence in decision making.

Theoretically at least, it is possible for a project for which total cost exceed total benefits to be worthwhile if it involves a redistribution in favour of the less wealthy. Indeed, much planned action is carried out with this effect. Decision rules B and C mentioned at the beginning of this chapter will only hold good if interpersonal comparisons of utility can be estimated.

The distributional implications are a central concern of

many planning projects. B.A. Weisbrod (1968) gives an interesting account of how implied weights for different groups of people may be calculated from decisions taken in the U.S.A. Lichfield's Planning Balance Sheets explicitly lists and evaluates as far as possible the effects of projects on all the groups of people who can be identified, an essential pre-requisite to estimating interpersonal comparisons of utility if not part of the estimation proper.

The choice of policy for shopping between allowing no conversions to other uses and allowing conversions to building societies will result in differences between the kinds of services and jobs created, and who is likely to benefit from them. The decision on which policy to adopt implies a choice between groups of users, potential employees and perhaps between mortgage applicants and shoppers as well as many more groups of people.

The difficulties of comparing benefits and costs to different people are compounded for long term projects because individuals and social and economic groups will change throughout the lives of the projects.

THE EVALUATION OF RISK

Uncertainty about the future is one of the fundamental problems of planning. The risk of inflation in construction costs or a fall in property prices are the main areas of uncertainty to the viability of a development project. In awarding tenders there will be the risk of development companies going out of business with a consequent increase in the cost of the project due to delay and to revisions in prices obtainable. Even for policies where no money changes hands between planner and those affected by the policies, there is always the risk of uncertainty as to what the effects of the policies will be. The example used earlier, of alternative policies towards the conversion of shops to other uses in Coventry Road Small Heath, depended on amongst other things, an estimate of the changes in the numbers and kinds of jobs which would be available in the premises affected. Problems of comparing these effects on different groups of employees and estimating the value of these jobs have already been explained in previous sections. There remains the problem of how to take account of the uncertainty of what the numbers and kinds of job will be. Is a 50/50 chance of getting a job in a building society worth half as much as 100% certainty? Probably not to most potential employees as the risk might prevent them taking measures to take up the job such as giving notice to leave a presently held job. Similarly, a 50/50 chance of 100 jobs will probably be valued less than certainty of 50 jobs.

The evaluation of risk becomes more explicit where money is involved. A project with costs of 2X will certainly be valued less than one where there is a 50/50 chance of the cost being X and a 50/50 chance of it being 3X. Amongst other reasons, planning can take place with certainty in the first case. Insurance is, of course, based on willingness to pay to avoid risks. The chances of a house being razed to the ground by fire are certainly less on average than the ratio of premium paid: sum insured. Otherwise the insurance company would soon go out of business. Nevertheless the premiums are paid to avoid risk from the point of view of the house owner, or to spread the risk viewed from the point of view of the insurance company.

The problems of risk for planning is two-fold. Firstly there is the problem of estimating the odds - what are the chances of property companies X and Y being unable to complete the contract? What are the chances of 100 jobs being lost in shops along Coventry Road? What are the chances of interest rates making the project uneconomic? These are formidable problems indeed. The methods of forecasting explained in chapter 6 may give some guidance. So too might statistical techniques of correlation analysis, regression and significance testing. Used sensibly and with a lot of questioning and reflection these will help to reduce the chances of being wrong but will certainly not eliminate them.

The second problem of risk in planning is that of valuing it. If we could be sure that there was a 50/50 chance of a project costing £X and a 50/50 chance of it costing £3X what cost are we to allow for it? Certainly more than £2X but how much more? The real dilemma arises when there is a choice between a project with costs of, for example, 50/50 chance of costs £X and another project with costs of 40/60 chance of costs £X - Y. Is the reduced cost worth the lesser chance of achieving it? In project evaluation generally, the practical problems are reduced if a market analogy can be found. In valuing risk, the market value can sometimes be estimating by reference to the insurance premium needed to cover it. The planner's valuation problem becomes the insurance company's. Unfortunately, only a fraction of the risks involved in planning can be insured.

CONCLUSIONS ON EVALUATION

In judging whether or not to go ahead with a planning project or policy or in choosing between alternative projects or policies, the problems of making a rational decision fall into four categories:

1) how to estimate costs and benefits at the time that they occur
2) how to take into account their occurrence at different times - estimation of discount rates
3) how to take into account the fact that they affect different groups of people, or how to estimate the values of benefits and costs to different people - interpersonal comparisons of utility
4) how to estimate the chances or probability of uncertain outcomes happening and how to value these probabilities after they have been estimated - the treatment of risk.

These four dimensions to the evaluation problem are indeed each formidable. They raise an almost infinite number of questions, most of which can not be answered satisfactorily. When applied in planning practice, these principles will provide a checklist to remind the planner of what questions are liable to be significant and a framework upon which they can be analysed systematically. The difficulty in applying them is in how to select which ones are important in deciding on the particular projects in hand - how to select the important questions in decision making and avoid spending a lot of effort on those not likely to effect the decision no matter what their value. Which questions are significant, of course, depends on the project, and each of those raised in this chapter will be significant in some circumstances.

The choice of technique used to present the findings is less important in arriving at the best decision. The choice between Lichfield's Planning Balance Sheet, Hill's Goal Achievement Matrix or any other approach is less important than the application of the principles involved in estimating the costs and benefits or disadvantages and advantages, although the method of presentation may be important in influencing the decision maker.

10 Monitoring and review

SITUATIONS FOR MONITORING AND REVIEW

In planning, monitoring is the act of keeping watch on all relevant factors in order to identify situations in which planning is needed. The 'relevant factors' are obviously the same as those which are deemed relevant in decision making which in turn are derived from objectives. Lists of objectives as written down in planning documents however, often omit many factors which are relevant to decision making presumably because they were thought too obvious to be spelled out, for example to minimise construction costs by avoiding steep slopes etc., to maintain the viability of shopping streets by resisting pressure for change to non-shopping uses.

Monitoring obviously depends on being able to describe through time the factors which influence planning decisions. It is the time element which is distinctive of monitoring. Information systems for monitoring must be able to account the information through time. Planning techniques which are good for monitoring are those which are good at taking into account change through time, for example threshold analysis. Techniques which are not much use for monitoring are those where the information relates to one point in time, for example development potential surface analysis. There can be no types of information or techniques which are exclusive to monitoring. Monitoring is simply the description of changes

138

in planning circumstances through time and the drawing of implications from them.

Monitoring should not be carried out separately from plan preparation. The trend away from 'end state' planning in recent years towards the view of planning as a continuous process has clearly resulted in more time and effort being devoted to monitoring. Generally, the greater the uncertainty and therefore the greater the need for flexibility, the greater the need for monitoring.

It is, of course, the duty of a local planning authority to keep under review the characteristics likely to affect the planning of their area. (Town and Country Planning Act 1971 S6; further advice is contained in DoE Circular 55/77). There are three main groups of circumstances in which review and policy formulation take place in local planning authorities. Firstly they can be the result of keeping watch on changes in the local situation or changes imposed locally from outside e.g. Central Government policies. Secondly they can result from changes in what a local planning authority tries to do - changes in their aims or objectives which may or may not accompany changes in local circumstances or changes in duties imposed on a local planning authority, for example responsibility for the homeless. Thirdly, review and policy formulation can take place automatically after a fixed period on the assumption that there will have been changes in local circumstance or objectives or at least such change is sufficiently likely to warrant review.

Several types of change locally can result in plan preparation or review of an existing plan:

Pressure for development A very common cause of local plan preparation or policy review is the receipt of an abnormally large number of applications for planning permission. These can be either applications for a particular kind of development in a vulnerable area such as the green belt fringe of a conurbation. In the first category may come for example, applications to change shopping to building societies in a main retail street. Many district planning authorities have experienced this kind of trend in recent years and as a result have prepared policy statements towards building societies, sometimes including perhaps banks and estate agents as well (the latter often running building society agencies). The reasons for preparing such a policy statement would usually be along the lines of:-

(i) concern for the loss of shopping and the effects that

gaps in the shopping frontage may have on those
retailers which remain,

(ii) uncertainty as to whether the changes are in the
interests of local residents - are more building
societies needed? - will they help unemployment? - what
effects will they have on rateable values and occupation
in the whole shopping street?

Another common area of concern in recent years has been the
conversion of premises for manufacturing industry to
warehousing, perhaps cash-and-carry warehousing. When this
occurs on a substantial scale, the local planning authority
may be persuaded to undertake a policy review to answer
questions such as:-

(i) how many jobs are lost by the change of use?

(ii) does this create a mis-match of jobs to local skills as
well as a decline in the total number of jobs?

(iii) what are the effects on the local and the wider economy?

(iv) will traffic be increased substantially, if so how much
and at what time?

A second type of pressure for development may be of several
sectors perhaps housing, industry, in an area which had not
previously been so attractive. Because of a previous lack of
attraction perhaps the local planning authority felt it
unnecessary to consider restrictive measures. The change,
however, would cause the need to reconsider, or review this
absence of policy.

Monitoring can therefore involve watching the progress of
indices representing objectives to give warning when some
critical threshold is approached or alternatively it can take
place to clarify the effects of a trend where uncertainty is a
cause for concern.

A change in the balance of the local planning system not
necessarily reflected in any physical form. A very
significant example for most of the U.K. in the early 1970s
was the rise in house prices. Another recent problem is high
unemployment. Sometimes the problems are so clear that no
formal monitoring is needed to become aware of them.
Sometimes, as the in the case of unemployment, the social and
other effects may be far from clear. Other problems are less
obvious; for example some kinds of inaccessibility to the

housing market or to social and welfare services. In all
cases a local planning authority will often see it as its duty
to keep watch on the situation with a view to helping solve a
problem not manifest in building terms by the provision of,
for example, housing or social facilities.

Some planning studies raise more questions than they answer
and indeed may be all the more valuable for doing so. For
example the preparation of a plan for an area of urban fringe
is very likely to raise the question of what kinds of land
uses best satisfy local needs - need for housing, recreation,
open space and so on. Thus some monitoring takes places as an
automatic conclusion of plan preparation. Preparation of one
plan often results in the monitoring of a range of factors
which could themselves be the subject of further studies.

Changes in policy from outside the local planning authority,
for example in Central Government Circulars. Invariably it
will be advantageous to monitor decisions of the agencies
which have the power to influence planning. Monitoring the
effects of these decisions on the ground may be too late as by
this time, commitment may be heavy and the possibility of
policy review limited.

Changes in the role of the planner Changes may be in either
the type of activities undertaken by the planner - their
duties - or the way in which they carry out their duties -
their objectives. Both may result from either internal causes
within the authority or be imposed from outside such as by
Central Government. Internal changes may result from for
example, a change in political make up following an election
or simply a change of mind perhaps resulting from some
pressure group. It is easy to think of practices which ten or
twenty years ago were accepted but which now are considered
harmful - high rise flats, large scale development, over-
enthusiasm for urban road building and so on.

Keeping a plan up to date Logically, every plan laying down
policies should be monitored until they are shown to be no
longer relevant and every plan laying down specific proposals
for development should be monitored until they are either
implemented or abandoned.

In the course of monitoring it is likely that policies and
proposals will be modified or new ones arise making monitoring
a continuous process. If policies and proposals are modified
then the proportion of time spent within a local planning
authority on monitoring would increase after initial plans had
been prepared covering the whole of their area. This seems to

141

have been the case in county planning departments following structure plan preparation. The use of monitoring in structure plans is explained in Floyd (1978).

METHODS OF MONITORING

Sources of information and Information Systems

Keeping information up to date is one of the chief problems in planning. A fair amount of information on population and housing is available regularly but for most other types of development, special surveys have to be carried out. Often these surveys will be impossible to keep up to date without repeating them, for example, most traffic surveys. In other cases however, for example recreation facilities, it will sometimes be relatively easy to have information collected during the normal administration of the recreation facility once it has been decided what information is required as a result of the initial survey.

Many data sources are facts rather than opinions - sometimes called 'hard data'. Particularly in monitoring, however, 'soft data' or opinions often arise unexpectedly. Newspapers, professional journals and attendance at committee meetings are all important sources of information in giving early warning of impending plan preparation.

One criterion in designing information systems is that they should be able to be kept up to date with a minimum of effort and expense in collecting information. It is attractive to relate information systems to information which is collected for other purposes - applications for planning permission, building control records, rating records. The potential of the computer in this field is formidable (see The Planner July/August 1982).

Planning techniques for monitoring

The best planning techniques for other purposes such as plan generation or evaluation are also useful when it comes to monitoring. The best techniques will have two qualities:

(a) They will lay out rationally the factors involved in decision making, so that the factors, their inter-relationships and the values encountered all have a clear meaning.

(b) They will take into account how the factors vary through time.

Both these qualities are necessary for an effective decision aiding technique whether it is used for monitoring or not. It is not possible to make an accurate estimate of present values without taking into account the way in which the factors involved in decision making vary through time. Benefits received at some time in the future are not as valuable as the same benefits received today.

Using planning techniques for monitoring therefore often shows up weaknesses for other purposes as well as monitoring.

SOME EXAMPLES

In monitoring and review of a project or policy there are three stages which should be carried out one after the other:

- measuring the relevant changes, for example the number of houses built, the changes in proportion of local residents who speak English, the changes in the number of shops along a main road. This step is straightforward and easy compared with the other two.

- separating out the effects of the project or policy from other factors which may have caused the changes observed. For example, to what extent is an increase in the number of local residents who speak English a result of the local education authority's recently introduced evening classes and to what extent is it a result of other factors such as increasing demands in language fluency from employers? The use of correlation techniques to measure the relationship between a policy and observed changes will be a first step in estimating the effectiveness. However, the same kind of correlation analysis should be applied between other possible causes and the observed changes. It may well be the case that a correlation between a policy and observed effects is purely fortuitous. Even after other possible causes have been examined it should be remembered that there is a clear distinction between correlation and cause (chapter 3). Using correlation analysis only reduces the area of uncertainty between the expected effects of a policy and observed changes.

- relating the believed effects of a policy to changes in the circumstances which gave rise to the need for the policy (review). If, at step 2, it was possible to estimate the effects of a policy, there is still the need to examine the desirability of these effects (and how they might change) within an environment which is itself continually changing. For example, suppose it was shown that a local education authority's evening classes in English have been effective in increasing the proportion of local residents who can speak English (a question addressed at the previous step above). There still remain the questions of whether these classes are the best way of achieving language fluency and whether they are still needed in their same form, given that more local residents speak English and with a greater degree of fluency.

Let us now look at how these three groups of questions might apply to two examples of policy monitoring.

Conversion of use of shops in Coventry Road, Small Heath (Birmingham) to other uses

In the previous chapter, two hypothetical policy alternatives were examined:

A) To refuse planning permission for conversions of shops to other uses

B) To refuse planning permission for conversions of shops to other uses except building society offices.

Let us examine some of the questions which might arise in monitoring and review of policy B.

Measuring the relevant changes - number, size, employment and type of shops lost; number, size of building society offices and jobs gained from shops, not from shops; estimate of the pressure for changes from shops to other uses; number of applications for planning permission refused, estimate of the effects of the policy in deterring the making of applications for planning permission; number of shops closed, jobs lost.

Separating the effects of the policy from other possible causes of the observed changes - How many shops could have been saved from closing by conversion to a use other than building society offices? How many jobs would have been retained? What would have been the effects on the Coventry Road shopping area as a whole? What are the social consequences? Has the policy resulted in an increase in local house building activity? What other factors might have contributed towards this?

Review of the policy Is there a need for further building

society offices? Would agencies in premises primarily for other uses such as estate agents or insurance brokers be an acceptable substitute? - to customers, for potential employees? Are shops in their present uses becoming more or less viable? Is the policy preventing shops from remaining in a beneficial use?

Classes in English for immigrants

Suppose a local education authority embarked on a policy of providing special tuition for local residents who could not speak English, perhaps with a view to raising levels of educational achievement and with other objectives discussed in chapter 8. What questions might arise in monitoring such a policy?

<u>Measuring the relevant changes</u> - changes in the number of proportion of English speakers; changes in levels of attainment in reading, writing and conversation. In addition to these direct changes, there would be many indirect ones perhaps of at least equal significance - for example levels of achievement in other school subjects resulting from greater ability in English, better job prospects and results, reduced cost of teaching in some other subjects where inability in English necessitates extra attention from teachers. Some of these indirect effects might have further consequences. For example better job prospects might result in a reduction in vandalism and other anti-social behaviour. What started as an apparently simple task of measuring changes in language ability actually opens up an almost limitless network of indirect effects.

<u>Separating the effects of the policy on English classes from other possible causes of the changes observed</u> Even the changes in ability in English could be the effect of many causes other than the policy adopted. Perhaps more jobs available where fluency in English is needed, increasing awareness of some sections of the immigrant community of opportunities outside - indeed many factors could cause similar effects. When we begin to examine the possible causes of the indirect effects of improvement in English language abilities, the number of factors liable to be significant is almost endless.

<u>Review of the policy</u> The previous step addressed the question of whether the policy has been effective. There now remains the question of whether it should be continued, modified or abandoned. This will involve examining such topics as whether the changes in ability in English support continuing the

present policy or replacing it by a different one, perhaps a different form of tuition, whether it should be aimed at different parts of the immigrant communities and whether the indirect consequences could be achieved more effectively by other means. In short, review of the policy implies an examination of the changes in the issues and needs which justified it and whether these show that policy change is needed.

CONCLUSIONS

The need for planning results from an attempt to solve problems or a desire to take best advantage of opportunities. Monitoring is the act of keeping watch for situations where these problems and opportunities arise. It is a preliminary to the preparation of policies and proposals in the sense that they follow when monitoring has shown such activities to be necessary. Monitoring also follows preparation of policies and proposals in order to ensure their continued relevance and desirability. Design of a methodology for monitoring should take place throughout the phases of plan preparation. Policies which cannot be monitored are almost as useless as policies which cannot be implemented. Monitoring is as important to a policy as a rudder is to a ship, whereas implementation is rather like the engine.

11 Changing uses for quantitative methods

What is expected of planners and the way they try to meet these expectations have been affected by a number of trends in recent years. Britain is not alone in experiencing the change in emphasis towards conservation and renovation and away from new-build (Kunzmann 1981, Ville de Lyon 1984, Dubedout 1978). Some of the methods included in previous chapters are quite specifically orientated to the planning of new developments and as a result, have declined in use in recent years. Examples are development potential surface analysis (chapter 7) and the gravity model (chapter 6). Other techniques have been adapted. Threshold analysis has been used as a method of analysing environmental capacities since at least the early 1960s but has been developed in this direction recently (Kozlowski 1982) rather than in its more common use in the 1960s and early 1970s as a method of analysing site costs for housing (chapter 7).

The trend away from new-build is perhaps a reflection of the increasing concern with environmental quality rather than quantitative targets. On the face of it, this may seem that a decline in use of quantitative methods would be inevitable. It has certainly coincided with a change in emphasis in the methods used. In times of a general decline in public and private spending the quest for cost-effectiveness and the planning effort might even be expected to increase. In fact a decline in investment may even create or intensify the kinds

of problems discussed in relation to Small Heath in chapter 8.
A decline in spending may create a need for more planning.

Of increasing concern for more than a decade have been the
problems of environmental protection. Stimulated by the large
scale projects of the 1960s particularly urban motorways, the
equal and opposite reaction did not take long to follow and is
still with us. Several countries including the U.S.A. and
France have legislative backing for environmental impact
studies with prescribed scope and context (Devaux 1977). In
Britain such studies are usually carried out by local planning
authorities or the Department of the Environment in a less
rigidly prescribed manner when they receive an application for
planning permission for a large project. They sometimes
involve a wide range of ecological and other criteria relating
to the natural environment as well as social and economic
factors. Nevertheless, the kind of evaluation criteria
reviewed in chapter 9 still hold in environmental impact
projects as well as cost-benefit studies.

Computers first came to be used significantly in planning in
the mid 1960s but until the late 1970s their use remained
largely in the hands of specialists. Programming and the use
of computers was relatively skilful. In most local
authorities it was centralised and access for everyday jobs
was not easy. Also their use was relatively expensive. For
more than a decade therefore they were used for only quite
specialised jobs and provided only a limited aid to manual
information systems. A useful review of the possibilities of
computers at this time was the June issue of the Town Planning
Institute Journal for 1970.

Micro-computers have been marketed in significant numbers
since the late 1970s. The size and cost are only a fraction
of main-frame computers and these are much easier to use than
the older machines. Programme languages have been simplified
so that almost anyone can use them using normal language.
Micro-computers can enhance the capacity to assemble, analyse
and synthesise data for a wide range of functions and are much
more efficient in terms of delivery.

System development has taken place in two main ways; in the
form of specific applications for a given function or task and
secondly as part of an integrated information system aimed at
increasing the co-ordination and efficiency of data handling
throughout the whole authority or firm. Integrated data
systems seem to be taking precedence in some local authorities
(see the special issue of The Planner July/August 1982
'Computers in Planning'). Their development depends on being

able to achieve three essential tasks:

A) establishing organising principles - data units, referencing systems for example,

B) creating data files to be linked to the information system

C) agreeing methods of keeping information up to date - for example procedures for co-ordinating data on change from building control, environmental health, housing departments and treasurers' departments.

The number of uses for computers as well as the number of authorities using them has proliferated since the late 1970s and still is increasing. The exact nature of these uses varies considerably from one authority to another depending on, amongst other things, the machinery used. However, generally, these uses have included the following:

1) Mathematical modelling and forecasting of two basic types - population models and many developments on the gravity model (chapter 6). Some of the best known early applications were of this type. Computers are particularly useful in sensitivity testing, which of course greatly multiplies the computing necessary beyond the original model.

2) Application of statistical methods such as using the Statistical Package for the Social Sciences (SPSS).

3) Digital mapping, for example of constraints on developments for application in development control.

4) Maintenance of an up-to-date register of all properties. The type of data on such a gazetteer varies according to requirements but commonly includes items such as, owner, occupier, address, land use, location (grid reference to 100, 10 or 1 metre), date of changes.

5) Ad hoc data files of change such as of land use, population or development completions (e.g. from sources such as Electricity Boards).

6) Processing of Building Regulations applications - recording progress, constraints, decisions.

7) Processing applications for planning permission. Often the County Council takes on the job of co-ordination, receiving data from the Districts and providing output for

local use as well as in Structure Plan monitoring and review. Generally such planning application systems are basically as follows:

   i)   Planning applications are received from Districts and sorted to determine which are relevant to the information system. Extensions to houses and other minor works of no strategic significance are excluded by many authorities leaving applications to erect new buildings and changes of use to enter the information system.

  ii)   Information on existing and proposed use, floorspace, number of residential units, expiry date of permission and other items is extracted.

 iii)   A few applications enter the system by gaining planning permission on appeal.

  iv)   Planning permissions leave the system or transfer within it when commencement and completion notices are received from Building Control Departments of District Councils.

8) The use of the word processor to avoid the repetition of much routine typing.

Changes in what is required of planners and the technology available to them can be expected to result in changes in the extent to which they use the various quantitative methods rather than the principles behind them. Better computers have enabled planners to use the same methods more efficiently, more effectively and more extensively. More rigorous data analysis is possible but still using the same basic methods.

If planning is to be effective in times of subdued demand or at least willingness to implement development there will be a need for a more co-ordinated effort between all the agencies able to influence urban policy - financial institutions and agencies and those responsible for taxation as well as land use and social development authorities. It seems doubtful whether this will cause any important changes in the use of quantitative methods beyond those already mentioned. The methods of presentation may change, but as long as there is an interest in rational decision making the same principles will remain valid.

In a book such as this, it has been possible only to give a glimpse of the complications of planning methodology. When these methods are applied there is a lot of scope for creativity - techniques are adapted to the situation in hand rather than applied mechanically. Applied without much imagination, planning technique will very likely lead to a lot of wasted effort pursuing solutions which were really non-starters and generally telling the decision maker what was already obvious. Even worse, they can hide in technical detail assumptions which are really value judgements from those applying them and can support rather tendentious conclusions. Applied with skill and imagination, planning techniques can complement the way decisions are made by drawing value free and unequivocal conclusions from data. These conclusions only help decisions rather than make them.

Bibliography

Albers, G. (1968) Toward a theory of urban structure, <u>Town Planning Institute Town and Country Planning Summer School</u>, 14-20.

Ascher, W. (1978) <u>Forecasting: An Appraisal for Policy-Makers and Planners</u>, John Hopkins University Press, Baltimore.

Atkins, L. (1979) <u>Causal Modelling</u>, in Block 7 of Research Methods in Education and the Social Sciences (DE304), Open University, Milton Keynes.

Barras, R. and Broadbent, T.A. (1979) The Analysis in English Structure Plans, <u>Urban Studies</u>, 16, 1-18.

Batey, P.W.J. and Breheny, M.J. (1979) Methods in Strategic Planning, Parts I & II, <u>Town Planning Review</u>, 9, 259-72 and 502-18.

Bather, N.J., Williams, C.M. and Sutton, A. (1975) <u>Strategic Choice in Practice: The West Berkshire Structure Plan Experience</u>, Geographical Papers 50, Department of Geography, Reading University.

Batty, M. (1970) An activity allocation model for the Notts/Derby sub-region, <u>Regional Studies</u>, 4.

Birmingham City Council (1976) <u>Small Heath Study & District Plan, Issues Report</u>.

Birmingham City Council (1980) <u>Inner City Partnership Programme</u> 1980-83.

Birmingham City Council (1981) <u>Small Heath District Plan, Written Statement</u>.

Blalock, H.M. (1972) <u>Social Statistics</u>, 2nd Edition, McGraw Hill, New York.

Booth, D. and Jaffe, M. (1978) Generation and Evaluation in Structure Planning, <u>Town Planning Review</u>, 149, 445-58.

Bovaird, A.G. (ed) (1978) <u>Economic analysis in local government</u>, JURUE, Aston University, Birmingham.

Bracken, I. (1981) <u>Urban Planning Methods</u>, Methuen, London.

Bracken, I. (1982) New directions in key activity forecasting, <u>Town Planning Review</u> 53, 1, 57-64.

Breheny, M.J. and Roberts, A.J. (1978) An integrated forecasting system for structure planning, <u>Town Planning Review</u> 49, 306-18.

Brunt, T., Abbott, C., Eatwell, C. and Downie, J. (1982) The Birmingham Envelope Scheme, <u>Housing Review</u> July-August, 130-33.

Bulmer, M. (ed) (1978) <u>Social Policy Research</u>, Macmillan, London.

Central Statistical Office (1984) <u>Social Trends</u> 1984, HMSO London.

Cheshire County Council (1976) <u>County Structure Plan, Report of Survey-Population</u>, Chester.

Clark, W.A.V. and Onaka, J.L. (1983) Life Cycle and Housing Adjustment as Explanations of Residential Mobility, <u>Urban Studies</u> 20, 47-57.

Cole, J.P. and King, C.A.M. (1968) <u>Quantitative Geography</u>, John Wiley.

Comrey, A.L. (1973) <u>A first course in Factor Analysis</u>, Academic Press, New York and London.

Cuthbertson, K., Foreman-Peck, J. and Gripaios, P. (1982) The Effects of Local Authority Fiscal Decisions on Population Levels in Urban Areas <u>Regional Studies</u> 16, 165-71.

Danson, M.W., Lever, W.F. and Malcolm, J.F. (1980) The Inner City Employment Problem in Great Britain 1952-76: a shift-share approach, <u>Urban Studies</u> 17, 195-210.

Dasgupta, A.K. and Pearce, D.W. (1978) <u>Cost-Benefit Analysis, Theory and Practice</u>, Macmillan, London.

Devaux, P. (1977) Les études d'impact (Impact studies), <u>Promotion Immobilière</u>, November, 57-63.

Draper, N.R. and Smith, H. (1981) <u>Applied Regression Analysis</u>, John Wiley and Sons, New York and Chichester.

Dubedout, H. (1978) La rénovation de l'habitat ancien est un problème national (The restoration of our environmental heritage is a national problem) in <u>Revue de l'Habitat Social</u>, 36, 29-41, Paris.

Essex County Council (1979) <u>County Structure Plan, Report of Survey</u>, Chelmsford.

Floyd, M. (1978) Structure Plan Monitoring, <u>Town Planning Review</u>, 49, 476-85.

Forbes, J. (1969) A Map Analysis of Potentially Developable Land, _Regional Studies_, 3, 179-95.

Frankfurt am Main Dezernat Planung (1976) _Generalverkehrsplan 76_ (Traffic Master Plan 76) Der Magistrat der Stadt Frankfurt am Main.

Friend, J.K. and Jessop, W.N. (1976) _Local Government and Strategic Choice_, 2nd edition, Pergamon, Oxford.

Gardner, G. (1978) _Social Surveys for Social Planning_, Open University Press, Milton Keynes.

Georgi, H. (1973) _Cost-Benefit Analysis and Public Investment in Transport: A survey_, Butterworths, London.

Haggett, P., Cliff, A.D. and Frey, A. (1977) _Locational Methods_, Edward Arnold, London.

Hakim, C. (1982) _Secondary Analysis in Social Research. A Guide to Data Sources and Methods with Examples_, George Allen and Unwin, London.

Hammond, R. and McCullagh, P.S. (1978) _Quantitative techniques in Geography_, Oxford University Press, London.

Harrison, A.J. and Quarmby, D.A. (1969) _The Value of Time in transport planning: a review_ in Theoretical and Practical Research on an Estimation of Time-Saving, European Conference of Ministers of Transport , Report of the Sixth Round Table, Paris.

Hickling, A. (1974) _Managing Decisions: The Strategic Choice Approach_, Mantec, Rugby.

Hickling, A. (1978) AIDA and the levels of choice in Structure Planning, _Town Planning Review_, 49, 445-58.

Hicks, J.R. (1939) The foundations of welfare economics, _Economic Journal_, December.

Hill, M. (1968) A goals achievement matrix for evaluating alternative plans, _Journal of the American Institute of Planners_, 34, 19-29.

Hope, K. (1968) _Methods of Multivariate Analysis_, University of London Press, London.

Hunt, H.J., Stanton, P.G. and Hodges, D. (1980) Getting an accurate forecast of local employment prospects, _The Planner_, 66.

Isard, W. (1960) _Methods of Regional Analysis_, MIT Press, Cambridge Massachusetts.

Isserman, A.M. (1977) The accuracy of population projections for subcounty areas, _Journal of the American Institute of Planners_ 43, 247-59.

Kaldor, N. (1939) Welfare propositions and interpersonal comparisons of utility, _Economic Journal_, September.

Kendall, M.G. (Ed) (1971) _Cost Benefit analysis_, English Universities Press, London.

Khakee, A. (1982) Urban Economics, Urban Geography and Planning, _Planning Outlook_ 25, 72-9.

Kirkbride, D.J. (1970) Employment demand projections and future land use requirements, *Journal of the Town Planning Institute*, 56, 213-16.

Kozlowski, J. (1968) Threshold Theory and the sub-regional plan, *Town Planning Review*, 39.

Kozlowski, J. and Hughes, J.T. (1972) *Threshold Analysis*, Architectural Press, London.

Kozlowski, J. (1982) *Threshold Approach to the definition of Environmental Capacity. A case study from the Tatry National Park in Poland*, Paper for the World National Parks Congress, Bali 11-22 October.

Kunzmann, K. (1981) *Das Tätigkeitsfeld Raumplanung* (The activity of spatial planning) in Studienfeld Raumplanung (The Discipline of Spatial Planning), Kunzmann K. and Nonnenmacher W. Institüt für Raumplanung, Universität Dortmund.

Lawley, D.N. and Maxwell, A.F. (1971) *Factor Analysis as a Statistical Method*, Butterworths, London.

Layard, R. (1973) *Cost Benefit Analysis*, Penguin, Harmondsworth.

Lee, C. (1973) *Models in Planning*, Pergamon, Oxford.

Lichfield, N., Kettle, P. and Whitbread, M. (1975) *Evaluation in the Planning Process*, Pergamon, Oxford.

Little, L.M.D. (1958) *A critique of welfare economics*, Oxford University Press, London.

Llewelyn-Davies, Weeks, Forestier-Walker & Bor (1974) *Birmingham Inner Area Study, Project Report*, Department of the Environment, London.

Llewelyn-Davies, Weeks, Forestier-Walker & Bor (1976) *Birmingham Inner Area Study, Housing Policies for the Inner City*, Department of the Environment, London.

Llewelyn-Davies, Weeks, Forestier-Walker & Bor (1977) *Birmingham Inner Area Study Educational Action Projects*, Volume 1, Department of the Environment, London.

Lynch, K. (1960) *The image of the city*, MIT Press, Cambridge, Massachusetts.

Lyon, Ville de (1984) *Ville de Lyon, Programme Habitat d'Initiative Publique. Propositions pour la période 1984-1989*, (City of Lyon, Programme of Public Environmental Works. Proposals for the period 1984-1989), Lyon.

Mansfield, N.W. (1971) The Estimation of Benefits from Recreation Sites and the Provision of a new Recreation Facility, *Regional Studies*, 5, 56-9.

Marsh, C. (1982) *The Survey Method. The contribution of surveys to sociological explanation*, George Allen and Unwin, London.

Martin, I. (1980) Do we need population forecasts? *The Planner*, 66, 2.

Masser, I. (1972) <u>Analytical Models for Urban and Regional Planning</u>, David & Charles, Newton Abbot.

Mishan, E.J. (1975) <u>Cost Benefit Analysis</u>, 2nd Edition, George Allen and Unwin, London.

Morgan, D.J. and Rudzitis, G. (1978) Predicting microlevel population change. <u>Geographical Review</u>, 68, 470-81.

Morriss, P. (1983) Should we subsidise public transport? <u>Political Quarterly</u>, 54, Oct/Dec, 392-8.

Morrison, D.F. (1976) <u>Multivariate Statistical Methods</u> McGraw Hill, London and New York.

Morton-Williams, J. and Stowell, R. (1974) <u>Small Heath Birmingham: A Social Survey, Birmingham Inner City Area Study</u>, Department of the Environment, London.

Murray, W. and Kennedy, M.B. (1971) Notts/Derbys: a shopping model primer, <u>Journal of the Town Planning Institute</u>, 57, 211-15.

Nachmias, C. and Nachmias, D. (1981) <u>Research Methods in the Social Sciences</u>, Edward Arnold, London.

Needham, B. (1971) Concrete problems not abstract goals, <u>Journal of the Royal Town Planning Institute</u>, 58, 317-19.

OPCS (1980) <u>Population Projections 1978-2018, Series PP2 No. 10</u>, Office of Population Censuses and Surveys, HMSO, London.

OPCS (1981) <u>Birth Statistics Series FM No 8</u>, HMSO, London.

OPCS (1982a) <u>Census 1981, County Report Leicestershire</u>, HMSO, London.

OPCS (1982b) <u>Mortality Statistics area</u>, HMSO, London.

OPCS (1982c) <u>Local Authority Vital Statistics Series VS No 9</u>, HMSO, London.

OPCS (1984) <u>Population Projections, Series PP3 No 5</u>, HMSO, London.

Openshaw, S. and Whitehead, P. (1978) Structure Planning Using a Decision Optimising Technique, <u>Town Planning Review</u>, 49, 486-96.

Oppenheim, A.N. (1966) <u>Questionnaire design and attitude measurement</u>, Heinemann, London.

Pearce, D.W. (1971) <u>Cost Benefit Analysis</u>, Macmillan, London.

Phelps, E.S. (ed) (1973) <u>Economic Justice</u>, Penguin, Harmondsworth.

Planner The (1974, April) Special issue on Futurology.

Planner The (1982, July/August) Special issue on Computers in Planning.

Pope, A.S. (1972) A new method of population projection, <u>Journal of the Royal Town Planning Institute</u>, 58, 265-9.

Press, S.J. (1972) <u>Applied Multivariate Analysis</u>, Holt, Rinehart and Winston Inc. London and New York.

Rhind, D. (ed) <u>A Census User's Handbook</u>, Methuen, London.

Richardson, H.W. (1969) <u>Elements of Regional Economics</u>, Penguin, Harmondsworth.

Roberts,M.(1974)An introduction to town planning techniques, Hutchinson, London.

Robertson, I. (1982) The measurement of population turnover, Town Planning Review, 53, 79-89.

Rose, E.A. (1984) Planning Today: a time for questions and reassessment, Journal of the Royal Town Planning Institute, 70, 9, 21-5.

Roth, G. (1967) Paying for Roads, Penguin, Harmondsworth.

Schreiber, A.F., Gatons, P.K. and Clemmer, R.B. (1971) Economics of Urban Problems, Houghton Mifflin, Boston.

Scottish Development Department (1973) Threshold Analysis Manual, HMSO, Edinburgh.

SETRA (1974) Urbanisme et Tranport: Les Critères d'Accessibilité et de Développement Urbain (Town Planning and Transport: Accessibility Criteria and Urban Development) Ministère de l'Equipment, Paris.

Simpson, B.J. (1975) The penalty point muddle, Town & Country Planning 43, 305-8.

Simpson, B.J. (1977) Some theoretical developments on threshold analysis, Urban Studies, 14, 79-88.

Simpson, B.J. (1983) Site Costs in Housing Development, Construction Press, London and New York.

Simpson, B.J. and Purdy, M.T. (1984) Housing on Sloping Sites: A Design Guide, Construction Press, London and New York.

Smith, B.M.D. (1976) What can Birmingham Metropolitan District Council do that will benefit the employment and economic situation in an inner area like Small Heath? A Personal Assessment to Stimulate Discussion, Working Paper No 45, Centre for Urban and Regional Studies, University of Birmingham.

Spiegel, M.R. (1980) Probability and Statistics, McGraw Hill, London and New York.

Stone, P.A. (1973) The Structure, Size and Costs of Urban Settlements, Cambridge University Press.

Tempest, I. (1982) Warehousing as an employment source - a study of employment density figures and local authority attitudes, Planning Outlook, 25, 105-10.

Thomas, P.G. and Moorcroft, E.E. (1977) People and houses of Cheshire 3. Client Group Estimation using a housing stock register. Research and Intelligence Section, Corporate Planning Unit, Cheshire County Council, Chester.

Thornley, A. (1974) Futurology and Structure Planning: Scenarios, Journal of the Royal Town Planning Institute, 60, 4, 642-5.

Turner, R. and Cole, H.S.D. (1980) An investigation into the estimation and reliability of urban shopping models, Urban Studies 17, 139-58.

UMRCC (1982) 1981 Census Data at UMRCC, University of Manchester Regional Computer Centre.

Wannop, U.A. (1972) An objective strategy: The Coventry-Solihull-Warwickshire sub-regional study, Journal of the Royal Town Planning Institute, 59, 159-67.

Weisbrod,B.A.(1968)Income redistribution effects and benefits - cost analysis in S.B. Chase Jr. (ed) Problems in Public Expenditure Analysis, The Brookings Institution.

West Midlands County Council (1977) Employment Densities Survey, Structure Plan Technical Paper, Birmingham.

Wright, S.R. (1979) Quantitative Methods and Statistics. A guide to social research, Sage, London.

Yates, F. (1981) Sampling Methods for Censuses and Surveys, Charles Griffin, London.

Yeomans, K. (1968) Statistics for the Social Scientist, Penguin, Harmondsworth.

Young, R.K. and Veldman, D.J. (1972) Introductory Statistics for the behavioral sciences, Second edition, Holt, Rinehart and Winston, New York.

Zarkovich, S.S. (1965) Sampling Methods and Censuses, FAO, Rome.

Index

development pressures, 138,
  139-40
digital mapping, 149
discount rates, 127,132-4
dispersal of development, 87
disposable income, 56
distance learning, 32
district plans, 97,107,111
Downie, J. 48
drainage, 91,93,132
Draper, N.R. 115
Dubedout, H. 147
durable goods, 74

East Anglia, 79-80
East Midlands, 59-61
Eatwell, C. 48
ecological validity, 17
ecology, 148
Economic and Social Science
  Research Council, 12
economic recovery, 9
economic welfare, 131-2
economies of scale, 72,130,
  132
education authorities, 31
education facilities, 11
educational achievement, 105
educational opportunities,
  31-3,38
elderly persons, 58,63,65,
  123,134
electricity supply, 87,91,
  93,128,131,139
employment density, 71
Employment, Department of,
  68
employment forecasting, 55,
  67-71
employment opportunities, 97
employment subsidies, 130
energy requirements, 56
English language, 105,107,
  143-6
enumeration districts, 38-9,
  66,76
Envelope Scheme, Birmingham
  40,48

Environment, Department of,
  80,139,148
environmental improvements,
  9,11,101
environmental pollution, 57
environmental potential,
  93-4,147
equal pay, 69
Essex County Council, 62
ethnographic research, 4,15,
  16,17,18
evaluation, 6,125-37
experimental research, 14,
  15,16,17,18
exponents, 72-7
external validity, 14,16,17,
  20

fares on public transport, 18
fauna, 93-4
fiscal policies, 1,2
flexibility, 139
flora, 93-4
Floyd, M. 142
Forbes, J. 89
forecasting, 2,5-6,18,19,24,
  28,55-77,117,119,149
Foreman-Peck, J. 64
France, 148
Frankfurt am Main, 23
free market, 86
Frey, A. 3
Friend, J.K. 79
frozen costs, 27-9,132
futurology, 80

Gardner, G. 54
gas supply, 87,91,93,131,132
gazetteers, 149
General Improvement Areas,
  40,48
Generalverkehrsplan,
  Frankfurt, 23
geographers, 3
Georgi, H. 126
goals, 22-4,28,81,111,113,
  125,126
Goals Achievement Matrix, 3,
  18,25,125,126,137

Gravity Model, 72-7,129,147, 149
green belts, 86,87,139
greenfield sites, 12,78
Gripaios, P. 64

Haggett, P. 3
Hammond, R. 3
Harris computer, 33-5
Harrison, A.J. 127
health authorities, 2,56
health centres, 23,93
heavy goods vehicles, 101
Hickling, A. 25,81
Hicks, J.R. 131
high rise dwellings, 23,141
Hill, M. 18,25,125,137
Hodges, D. 70
Hope, K. 115
hotels, 93
house prices, 65,123,129, 140-1
household forecasting, 63-65
Housing Action Areas, 40,48
housing amenities, 38
housing associations, 2,9, 12,64,122
housing authorities, 23
housing conditions, 107-110
housing costs, 89-93,129,147
housing density, 86-89
housing forecasting requirements, 55,66
housing sites, 9
housing tenure, 38
housing treatment, 40-54
Howard, E. 87
Hughes, J.T. 25,89,91
Hunt, H.J. 70
hypotheses, 5,8-12,13,18,19, 20,31-9,123

immigrants, 107,123,146
implementation, 6,28,29,146
income tax, 130
industrial floorspace, 65
industrial location, 3,40-54, 128
industrial renovation, 1

industrialists, 101,128
information collection, 24, 138,142
infrastructure 90,93-4, 101, 119,128
insurance, 136
Input-Output Analysis, 3,25, 68-9
intangible costs, 27,127-8
interest rates, 132-4
internal validity, 13-14,20
inter-personal comparisons of utility, 13,134-5
interviews, 15
Isard, W. 69
Isserman, A.M. 58
issues, 2,3,4,6,7-8,13,18, 20,31-3,95-107,115,117,123

Jaffe, M. 125
Jessop, W.N. 79
job prospects, 31,32,38,69, 112,113,115,127,140,144, 145
journey to work, 23,73,76,88

Kaldor, N. 131
Kendall, M.G. 126
Kennedy, M.B. 75
Kettle, P. 25
Khakee, A. 2
King, C.A.M. 3
Kirkbride, D.J. 70
Kozlowski, J. 25,78,89,91, 147
Kunzmann, K. 147

labour costs, 130,131,132
labour force, 105
land acquisition, 4,37
land analysis, 89-94
land use forecasting, 57, 70-1
land use planning, 1,2,119
land use surveys, 3
landscape values, 14,27,93
language problems, 105,107, 111,113,115
Lawley, D.N. 115

Layard, R. 127,131
layouts of development, 30
Lee, C. 73
Leicestershire, 59-63
Lever, W.F.
Lichfield, N. 18,24,125,135,
    137
light industry 71
linear cities, 88-9
linear regression, 66
Little, I.M.D. 131
Llewelyn-Davies, Weeks,
    Forestier-Walker and Bor,
    planning consultants, 111,
    123
local authorities, 12,65
local education authorities,
    105
local government, 56,131
local planning authorities,
    22-3,24,139,140,141,148
local plans, 64,95-124
location quotient, 3,68
Lynch, K. 24
Lyon (France), 147
mail order shopping, 11
mainframe computers, 148
Malcolm, J.F. 70
Manchester, University of,
    33,34
manpower planning, 2,94
Mansfield, N.W. 127
manufacturing industry, 70,
    71,140
mapping techniques, 3
marginal costs, 91,129-30,
    134
market values, 128-32
Markov theory, 79
Marsh, C. 12
Martin, I. 57
Masser, I. 69
mathematic models, 25,149
Maxwell, A.F. 115
McCullagh, P.S. 3
metal manufacturing
    industry, 71
micro-computers, 148-50
migration, 32,33,62-3,64

Mishan, E.J. 126
model settlements, 86-9
monitoring, 6,28,29,138-46,
    150
monopolies, 131
Moorcroft, E.E. 67
Morgan, D.J. 64
Morrison, D.F. 115
Morriss, P. 126
mortgages, 127,135
Morton-Williams, J. 105
motorways, 148
Murray, W. 75

Nachmias, C. 54
National Economic
    Deveopment Council, 68
National Institute for
    Economic and Social
    Research, 68
National Insurance
    Contributions, 130
Needham, B. 81
Newton, Sir Isaac, 72
new towns, 78,79,86-9
noise, 128
normal distribution, 50-1
nucleated settlements, 88
null hypothesis, 46

objectives, 22-4,28,78,111,
    113,138,139
Ojectives Compatibility
    Matrix, 23,24
observation, 15
obsolescence of planning
    techniques, 5
obsolescent land, 111
Office of Population
    Censuses and Surveys, 34,
    59-61
offices, 9,65,70,86
Onaka, J.L. 65
Openshaw, S. 79
Open University, 32
operational aims, 12
Oppenheim, A.N. 54

164

sampling, 3,14,25,54
Sandwell Metropolitan
  District, 36
scales of measurement, 20
scatter, 3,80
scenarios, 80
schoolchildren, 31-9
schools,23,31-9,57,63,91,
  111,114,117
Schreiber, A.F. 126
Scottish Development
  Department, 91
second best, 131-2
sensitivity testing, 149
service industries, 67-8
servicing costs, 89,131,132
SETRA, 129
setting of research, 4,15,16
  17,18
shared dwellings, 109
shopping, 86,101,102,103,105
  111,117 126,135-40,143
shopping forecasting, 55,56,
  57,73-7
sieve maps, 89-90,91
site selection, 13,22,27,147
sixth formers, 31-9
sloping land, 90,91,93
small area statistics, 34
Small Heath, Birmingham, 95-
  124,126,128,130,131,135,
  136,144,148
Smith, B.M.D. 101
Smith, H. 115
Snedecor's Variance Ratio
  Test, 52
social goods, 131
social indicators, 14
social services, 2,105,109
socio-economic groups, 38
soil instability, 93-4
Solihull, 36
solution tree, 84-5
South Hampshire Study, 70-1
Sparkbrook, Birmingham 40-
  54, 96
Spearman's Rank Correlation
  Coefficient, 50-1
Spiegel, M.R. 115

sports facilities, 55
standard amenities, 107
standard deviation, 34,35,51
  52,53,107
Stanton, P.G. 70
statistical associations, 17
Statistical Package for the
  Social Sciences, 66-7, 149
statistics, literature on, 3
statutory town and country
  planning, 1,2,21,23,26,124
stereotypes, 78,86-9
Stone, P.A. 65,71
Stowell, R. 105
strategic choice approach,
  79
structure plans, 4,64,79,80,
  125,142,150
Structure and Local Plans
  Regulations, 26
Student's t test, 29,35,36,
  51-2,53
subjectivity in planning, 30
sub-regional plans, 25-6, 78
subsidence, 91,101,
subsidies, 69
survey research, 14-18
Sutton, A. 80
Sutton Coldfield, 36
systems planning, 57

taxation policies, 1,69,
  130,131,150
tax payers, 31
tax relief, 130-1
teachers' attitudes, 38
techniques in decision
  making, 4,5
techniques of planning, 2-4
technological change, 70
Tempest, I. 71
tenders, 135-6
Thomas, P.G. 67
Thornley, A. 80
Threshold Analysis, 3,12,15,
  25,29,79,89,91-4,138,147
time, value of, 127,128
time discounting,13,132-4,
  143

tourism, 93-4
Town and Country Planning
  Act 1971, 64,124,139
town expansion, 23,79
town planners, 86
traffic, 43,50,89,140
traffic surveys, 14,142
transport authorities, 26
transport planning, 2,4,8,
  10,18,23,26,56,74,86-9,
  94,129
travelling costs, 86-7,127
  -8,129
trend forecasting 57-8,61,
  63
Turner, R. 77

uncertainty, 27,117,119,135-
  6,140
unemployment, 32,130
urban design, 9
urban farm, 118
urban growth, 78,86-9,90,91
USA, 148

vacant land, 64,116,118,119
Vale Royal, Cheshire, 67
vandalism, 9
VAT, 130
Veldman, D.J. 53

Wannop, U.A. 89
ward data, 33-9
warehousing, 70,71,128,140
water supply, 87,91,93,131,
  132
water tables, 93
Weisbrod, B.A. 135
West Berkshire, 80
West Midlands County
  Council, 71,101
Whitbread, M. 25
Whitehead, P. 79
Williams, C.M. 80
word processors, 150
women in employment, 69
Wright, S.R. 53,115

Yardley, Birmingham, 97

Yates, F. 54
Yeomans, K. 53,115
Young, R.K. 53

Zarkovich, S.S. 54